JOY!

JOY!

Photographs of Life's Happiest Moments

BRUCE VELICK Introduction by Robert Emmons, PhD

CHRONICLE BOOKS
SAN FRANCISCO

Library of Congress Cataloging-in-Publication Data available.

ISBN: 978-1-4521-6789-3

Manufactured in China.

FSC
www.fsc.org
MIX
Paper from responsible sources
FSC™ C104723

Designed by Domino Design

10 9 8 7 6 5 4 3 2 1

Chronicle Books LLC
680 Second Street
San Francisco, California 94107
www.chroniclebooks.com

FOR DENISE . . .

"To get the full value of joy
you must have someone
to divide it with."

—MARK TWAIN

FOREWORD

I'm a curator by trade, not a writer; my gallery walls hang between the covers of this book.

After having looked at thousands and thousands of images and selecting those for the book, one of the great joys of a curator is how the images are arranged, how they talk to one another. Or, as I like to think, how they **hang** together. While each image was chosen on its own merits, I love how the pairings show the universality of a smile and a feeling of joy.

The images collected here come from photographers from around the world—China, France, Greece, England, Iran, Austria, and the United States. They include many of the world's best-known photographers and the dates the images were taken range from the early 1920s to the present.

I hope you enjoy the exhibition as much as I have enjoyed hanging it.

—BRUCE VELICK

AN INTRODUCTION TO JOY

ROBERT EMMONS

We were born for joy. This capacity is factory-installed. It is not optional equipment, an after-market add-on.

Yet joy can be difficult to talk about. Personal, private, and powerful, the topic can be a conversation stopper, too intense for polite exchanges, and too hard to define. Mere words may fail us, but we cannot ignore it.

One way to express joy is through the medium of art. Bruce Velick exquisitely captures this emotion throughout this beautiful and elevating book—a collection of joyful images depicting joy in lived lives. We may not know how to define joy, but we know it when we see it.

Why is joy important? Joy matters. It is vital to well-being. No serious discussion of human flourishing is possible without a consideration of the nature of joy and its place in the good life. It is one of those qualities that makes life most worth living. Without joy, life would be flat, unidimensional, monochrome.

Joy is fundamental to human existence and well-being. "We cannot understand human beings unless we understand joy and how joy comes to be," wrote famed Harvard psychiatrist George Vaillant. By giving expression to our ecstatic nature, joy points beyond itself to something deeply true about human nature and purpose. In true joy, our souls are opened, giving our existence a certain fluidity, a sense of easiness.

Though we may intuitively realize that joyful lives are better lives, that we function more effectively and feel best when our lives have frequent doses of joy, it does not follow that we know how to make joy happen.

Nor, on a clinical level, do we necessarily know exactly what joy is. Joy is the last major unexplored positive emotion, largely neglected by scientists who research human emotions. Why is this? Perhaps it's seen as redundant with happiness. Researchers have rarely distinguished between happiness and joy, and this lack of differentiation has hindered progress. My earliest research was in the psychology of happiness—who is happy, and why? The scientific field of happiness has made great strides in recent decades, but it has taught us little about the emotion of joy. After all, joy and happiness are not the same thing.

JOY IS NOT HAPPINESS

Joy is more intense than happiness. It almost always involves connection with forces outside ourselves: it is generally not under our own power to create or induce. Joy can happen even in the midst of suffering. It is spiritual whereas happiness is secular. Happiness is based on happenings, but joy is a way of being in the world. In joy, all things are bigger, bolder, and brighter.

Joy is a transformation involving the opening of the heart, a reconnection with a power greater than ourselves. Joy has to do with reading the world as a gift; as good (now or in the future); as abounding and overflowing; as a place of connection with the sources of goodness. It connects us to a larger reality, and it is right at the heart of what it means to be fully alive.

Joy not only helps to make life worth living for people, it can motivate people to give of themselves for the good of others. Joy provides an uplifting sense of goodness that can sustain other virtues, contributing to a truly flourishing life.

So, unlike happiness, joy is not primarily all about us. Psychologist Edward Hoffman and his colleagues asked respondents to describe a recent joyful experience. Experiences of interpersonal connection were reported by far the most frequently, outnumbering all other categories combined. Some of the joy-producing experiences frequently reported were the birth of a child or grandchild, family togetherness, recovery of a family member from illness or accident, romantic bliss, the wedding of an adult child, caregiving to a nonfamily member such as mentoring or volunteer work, and vicarious achievement (i.e., parental pride in a child or grandchild's accomplishment).

We see these powerful themes of interpersonal connection on display throughout the marvelous book you now hold in your hands. Joy seeks company. And the company of the joyous feeds the joy of each. When in joy, we want the experience magnified and amplified, and other people help make this happen.

Perhaps the most vital difference between joy and happiness is that joy can, counterintuitively, be linked to pain and suffering. Joy does not deny the reality or depth of suffering that are also a part of life. Rather, the joyous person affirms and admits that joy is often born out of deep suffering. Think of the joy on occasions normally associated with grief, such as a funeral or a memorial service. The joy here comes from reunion with friends and relatives of the departed one, as well as from remembering and celebrating the life of the departed. The novelist Frederick Buechner wrote that "joy is a mystery because it can happen anywhere, anytime, under the most unpromising circumstances, even in the midst of suffering."

Because those who feel intense positive emotions also often feel intense negative emotions, opening oneself up to joy also opens one up to suffering. Beethoven's pain gave us "Ode to Joy." Joy in the midst of life's challenges can help us to be courageous and see beyond our momentary troubles. It can draw our focus to the big picture and remind us that there is a transcendent reality—that which is called God in many traditions—and that we can have a relationship with that reality.

Joy carries a sense of the unexpected, of surprise. It often involves both memory and longing. The theologian C. S. Lewis wrote in his memoir, **Surprised by Joy**: "All joy reminds. It is never a possession, always a desire for something longer ago or further away or still 'about to be.'" In this sense, joy indicates something deeper, more embodied, more acute—it is akin to aliveness, or an animating force. According to Lewis, joy "must have the stab, the pang, the inconsolable longing."

WHAT IS THE FUNCTION OF JOY?

All emotions, joy included, are hardwired in our brains for a reason. What is the evolutionary purpose of joy? Joy, along with other social emotions such as gratitude, love, forgiveness, compassion, and trust, permit human beings to find and bind close to one another, to function more fruitfully, and ultimately to survive more successfully.

Joy is emotional equipment that drives the attachment system in children and their parents. This system is present in all mammals and is designed to keep dependent infants close to their mothers until they are sufficiently mature to survive on their own. Think of the joy you experience when you reconnect with a loved one after a period of separation. Visit any airport and observe returning travelers being reunited with their families. Pure joy. Because joy is induced by the reunion that follows separation, it is the anticipated and then realized joy that reinforces the return to the attachment figure.

When we are children, the attachment figure is our parent. For adults, it is likely to be a romantic partner. Joy is the primary neural reward system dedicated to separation and return. The promise of joy incentivizes us to attach, and to return to the object of our attachment. Throughout history, the capacity for joy has provided a powerful selection advantage for the survival of children. Again quoting George Vaillant, "A powerful reward system is needed to retrieve them from freeways and tigers, especially if it takes ten to twenty years to grow up."

JOY AND THE HUMAN SPIRIT

As it connects us outward and upward, joy is spiritual. Devotional writers have long located the emotion of joy within the human spirit. The Dalai Lama, Archbishop Desmond Tutu, Rabbi Jonathan Sacks, among other spiritual giants, prefer the term joy over happiness. Joy is part of the very essence of human nature, intrinsic to what it means to be human.

The philanthropist Sir John Templeton believed that joy was one of the key virtues and thematic organizing principles of life. He wrote, "Have you ever noticed how some people seem to be joyful no matter what is going on in their lives?" Real joy is a deep and lasting quality that helps transcend difficulties and restores a zest for life and living no matter what happens. For scientist and Jesuit priest Pierre Teilhard de Chardin, joy was the most infallible sign of the presence of God. The famous account of Blaise Pascal's dramatic spiritual transformation is saturated with "joy, joy, joy tears of joy . . . Eternally in joy . . ."

One thing we have learned from a scientific analysis of joy is that there is no clear or easy definition of what it may be. Nor can it be analyzed from a single disciplinary vantage point, whether brain science, evolutionary biology, the psychology of emotion, or theology and other humanities. No, it is too big to fit neatly into a disciplinary box. In the study of joy, the sciences and the humanities must marry.

Ultimately, we must do more than simply talk about joy. We must experience it. Joy may be hard to define, but we know it when we have it, and we know it when we lose it. Robert Louis Stevenson got it right when he said, "and the true realism, always and everywhere, is that of the poets: to find out where joy resides, and give it a voice far beyond singing. For to miss the joy is to miss all." Let's not miss it. Let's turn the page and experience joy for ourselves.

References

Lama, Dalai, Desmond Tutu, and Douglas Abrams. **The Book of Joy: Lasting Happiness in a Changing World**. New York: Avery, 2016.

Lewis, C. S. **Surprised by Joy: The Shape of My Early Life**. New York & London: Harcourt Brace, 1955.

Stevenson, Robert Louis. "The Lantern-Bearers." In **The Lantern-Bearers and Other Essays**, edited by Jeremy Treglown (pp. 226–235). New York: First Cooper Square Press, 1999.

Templeton, John. **The Essential Worldwide Laws of Life**. West Conshohocken, PA: Templeton Press, 2012.

Vaillant, George. **Spiritual Evolution: A Scientific Defense of Faith**. New York: Broadway Books, 2008.

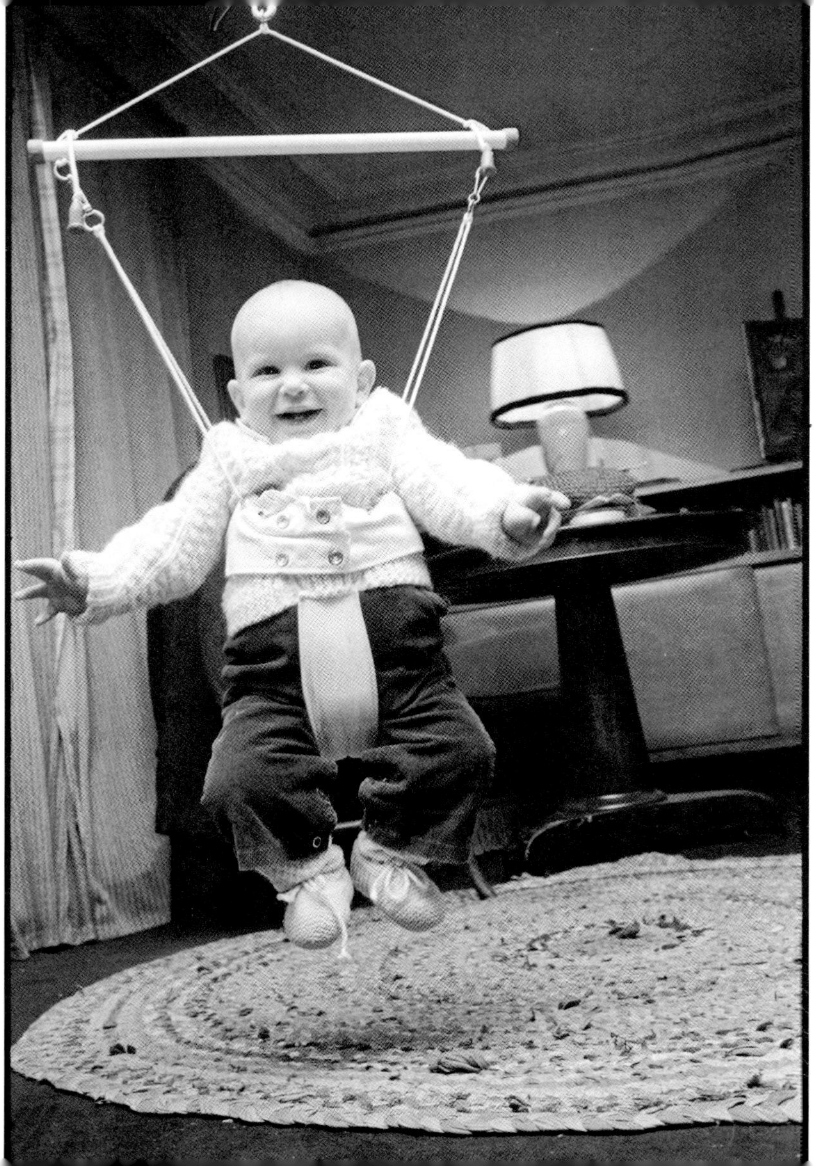

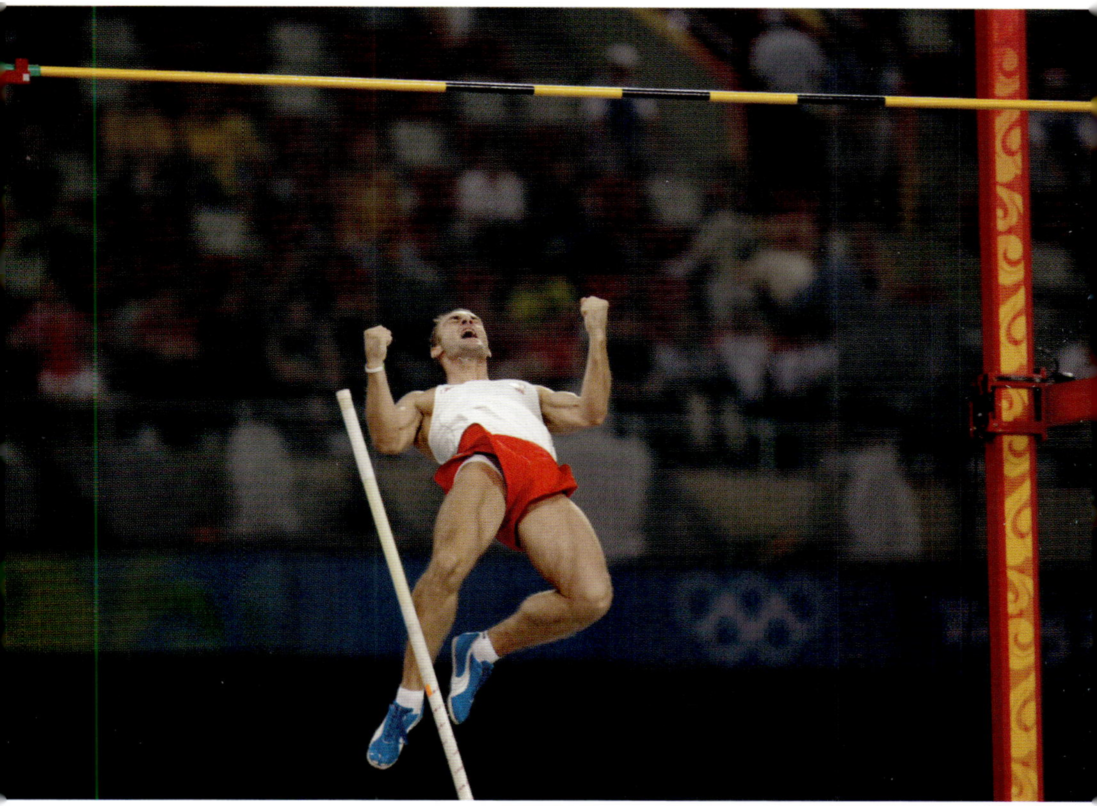

1 2

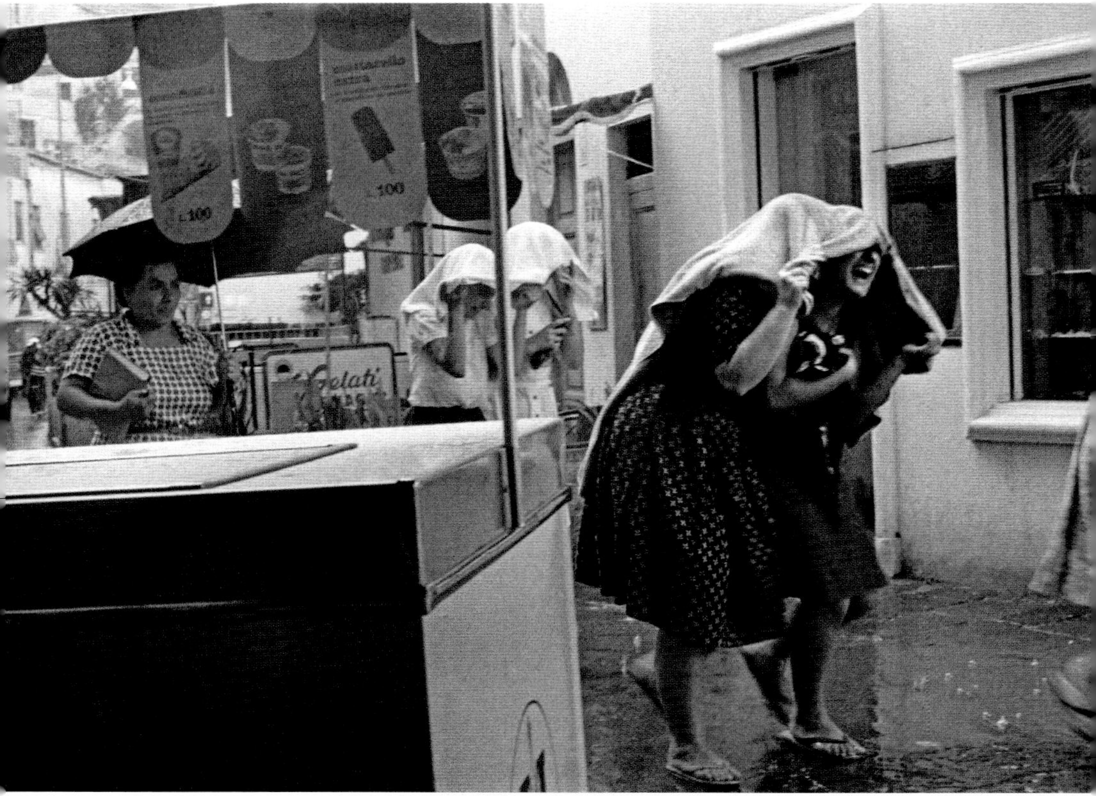
Gelati

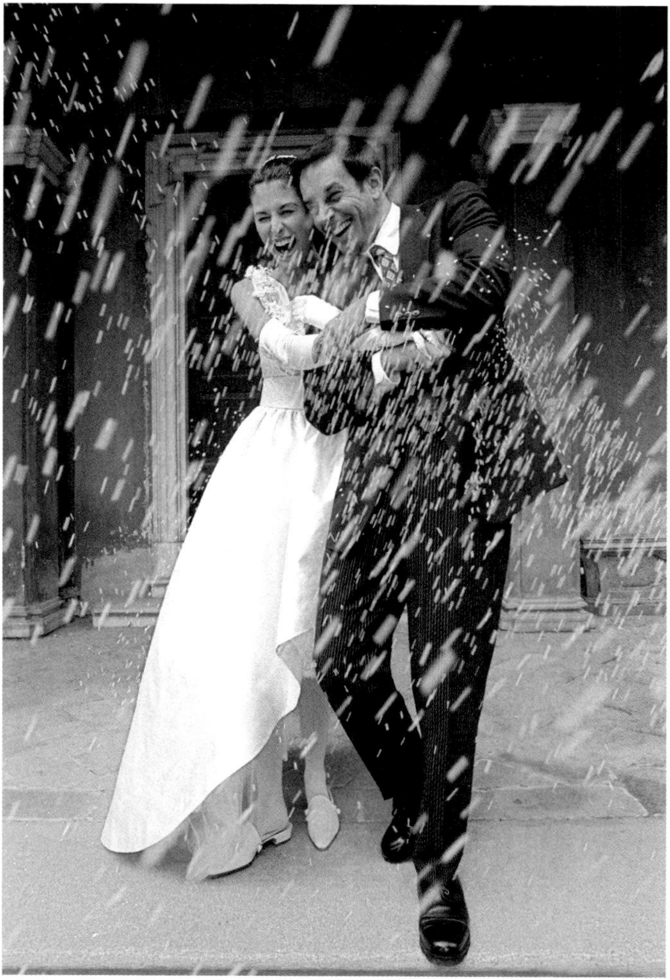

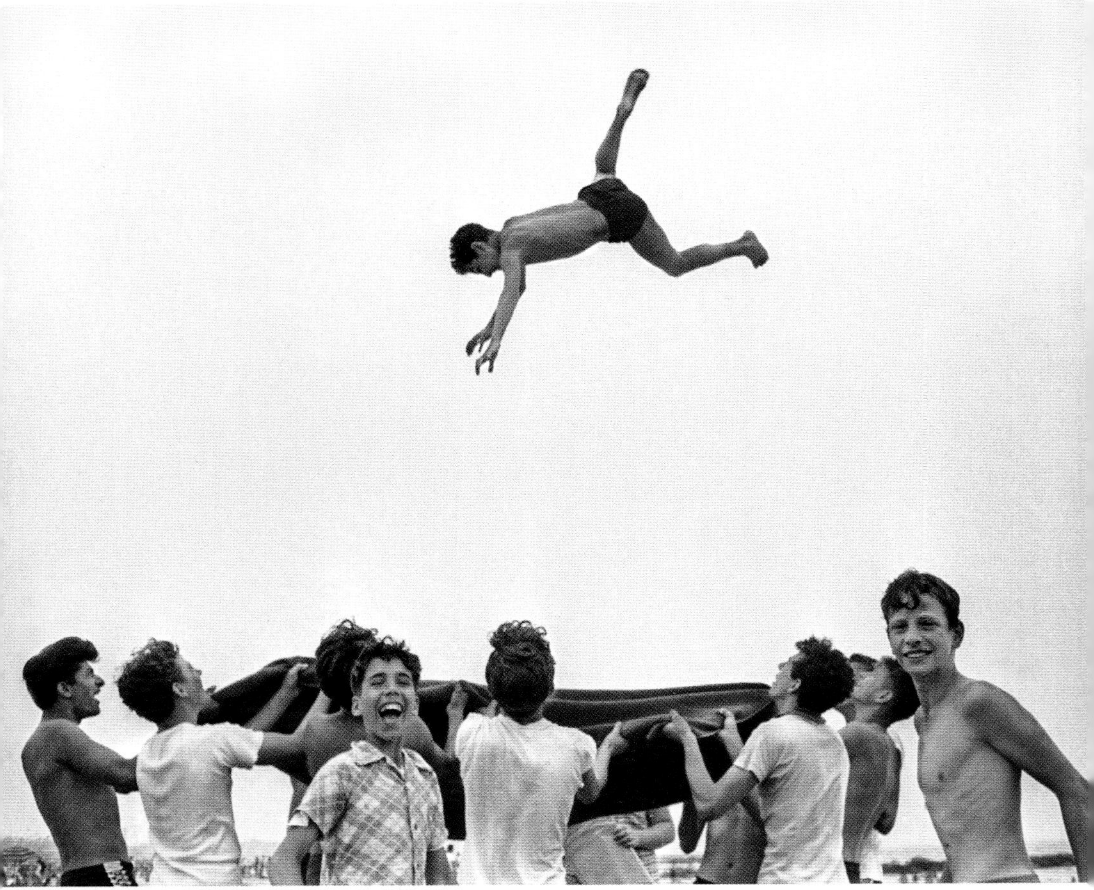

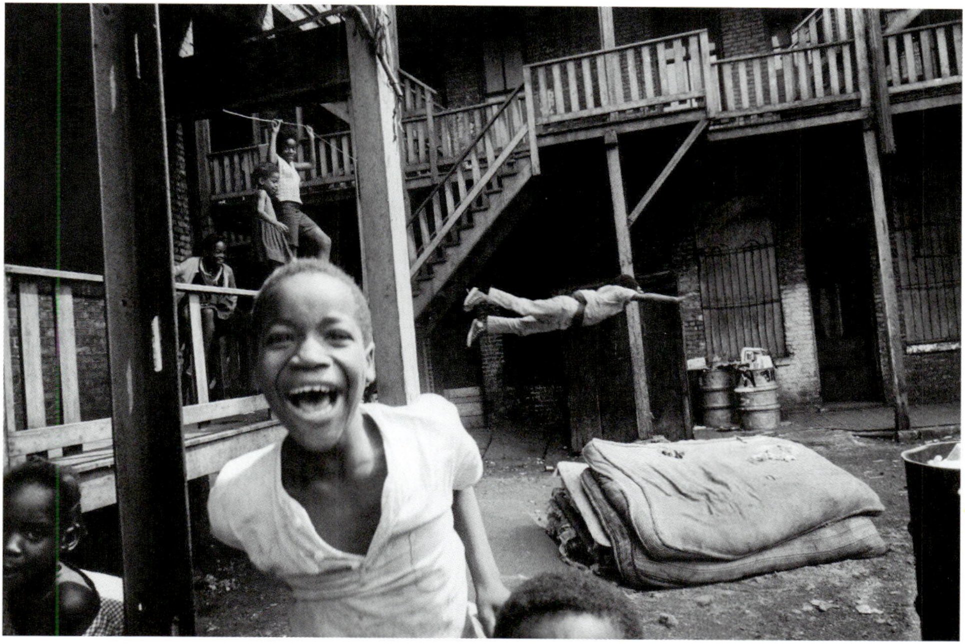

5

6

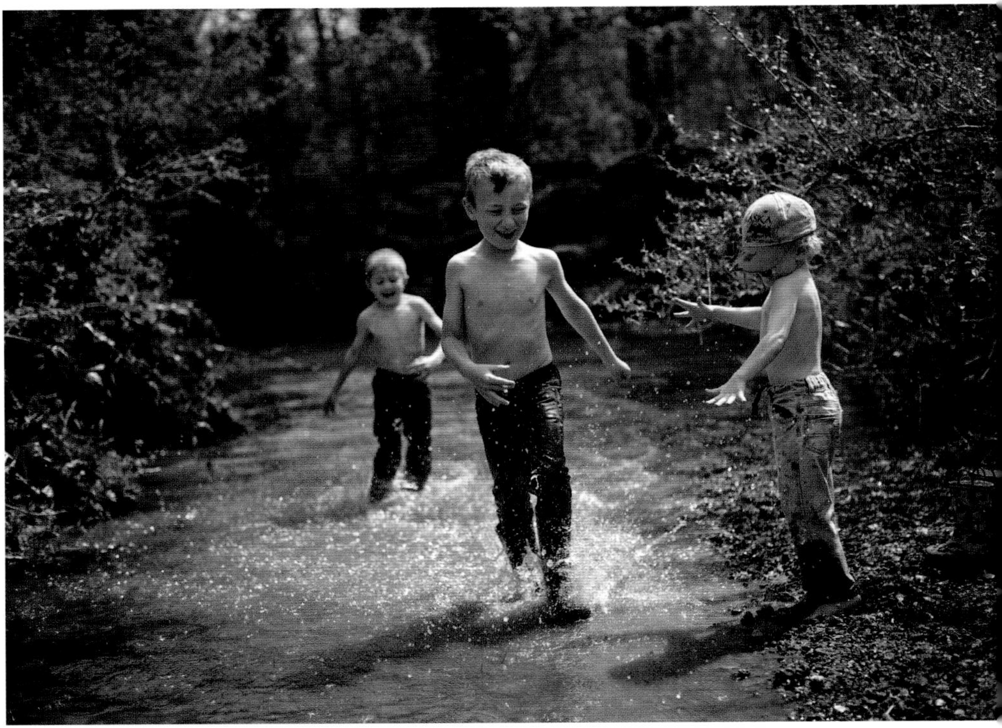

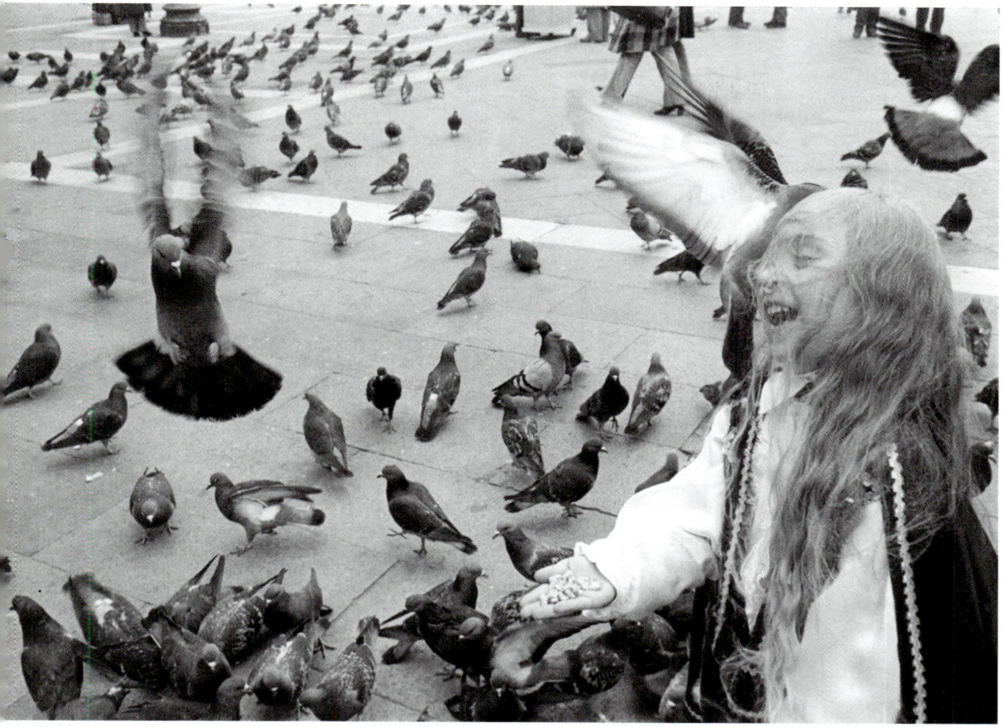

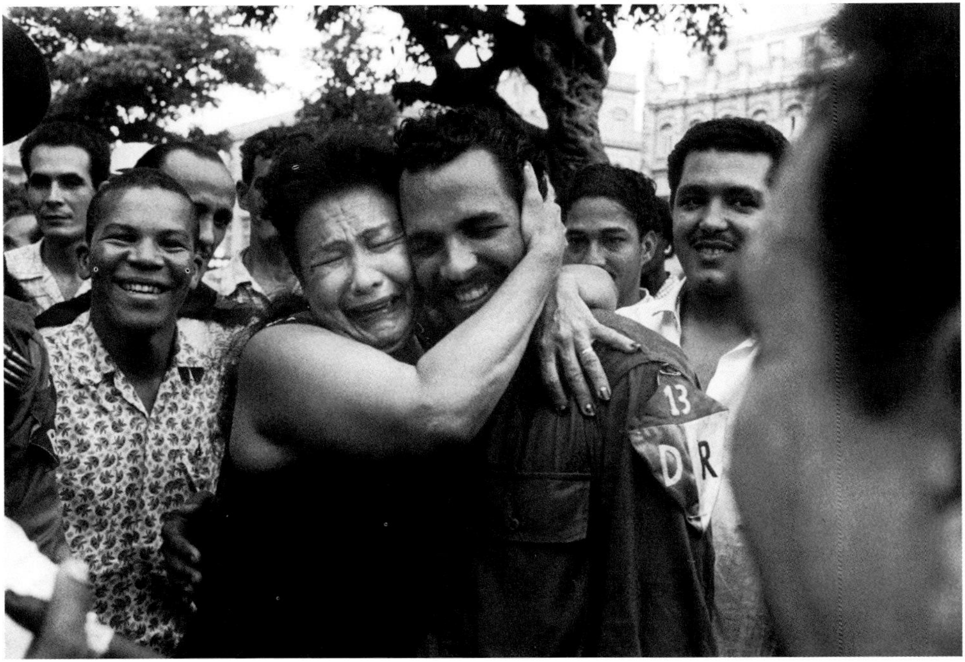
13
D R

The pain of parting
is nothing to the joy
of meeting again.

CHARLES DICKENS

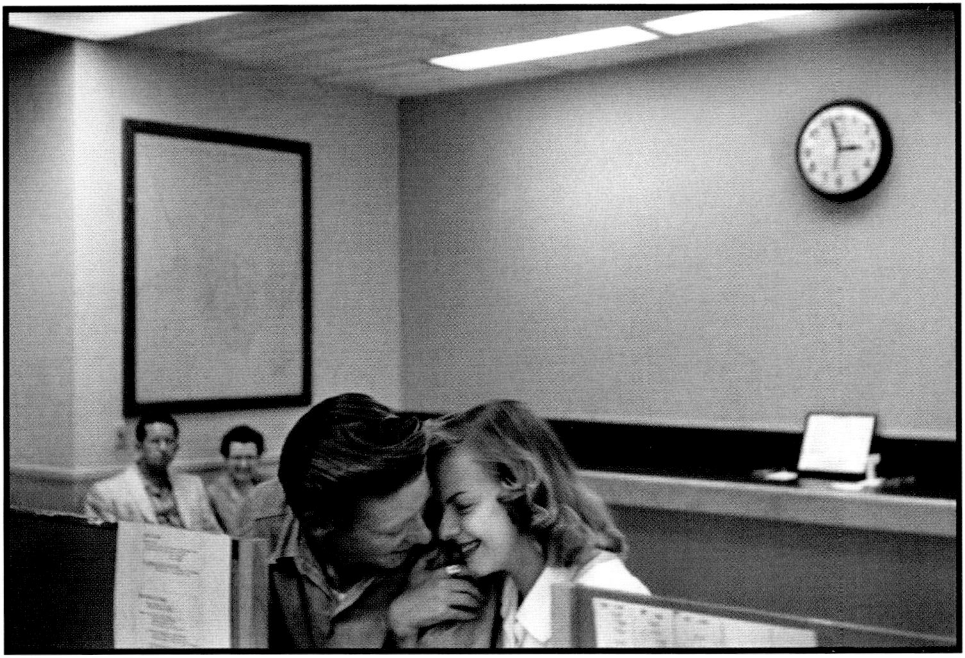

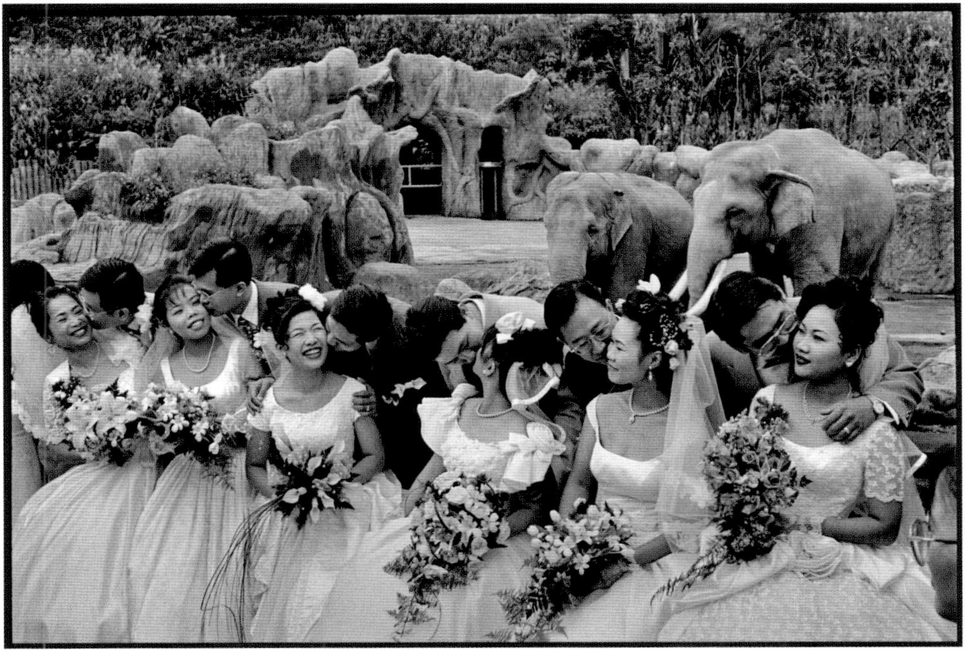

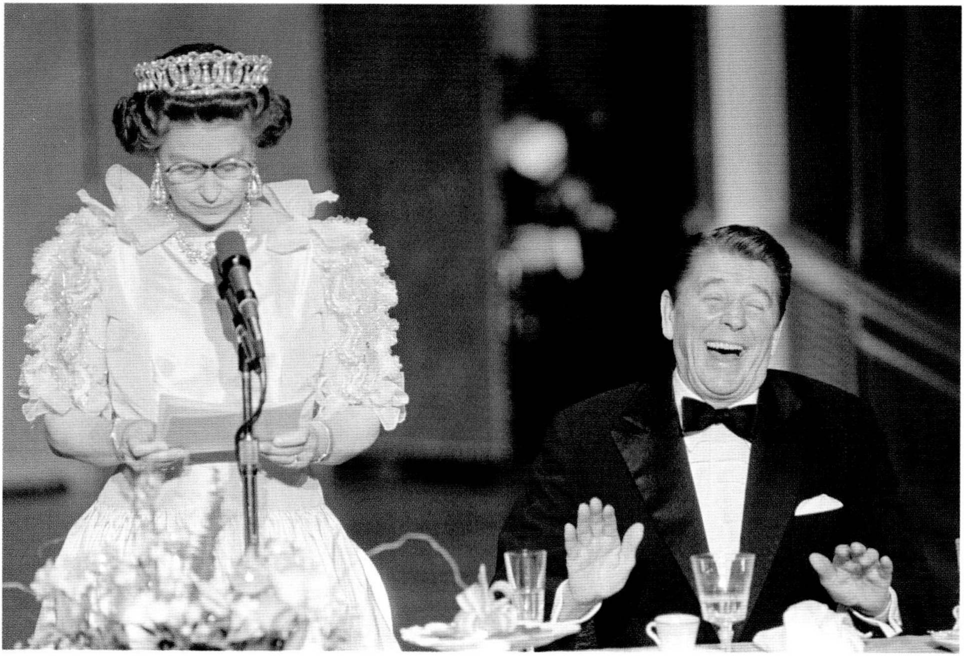

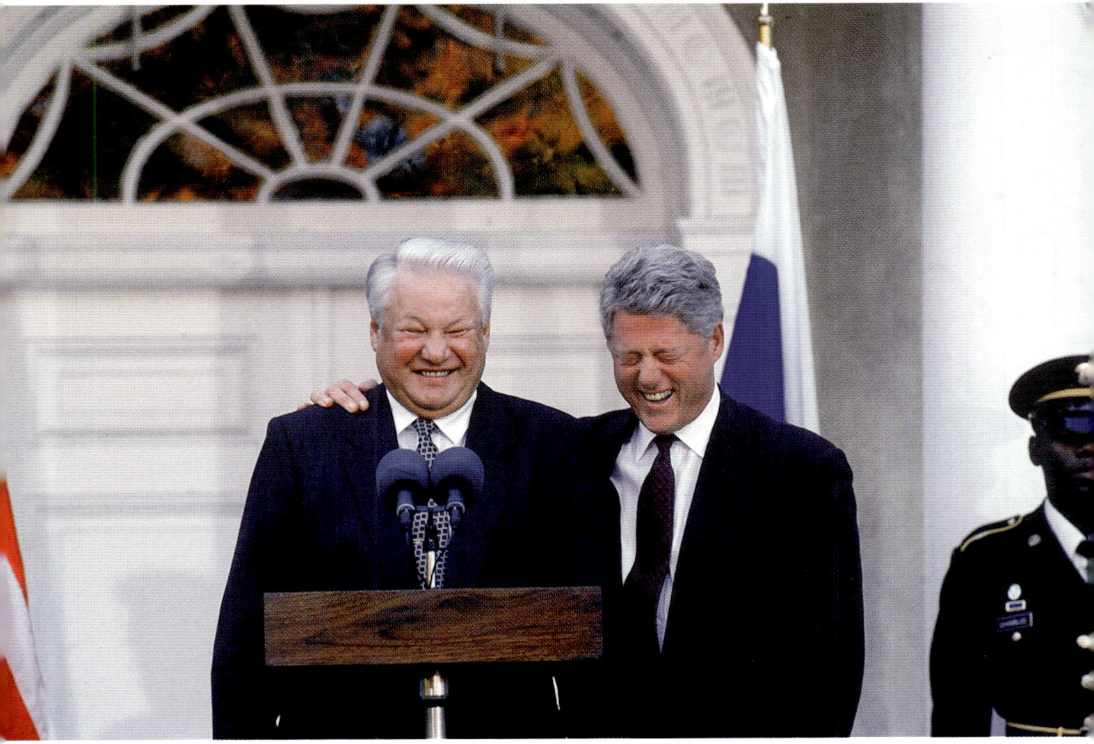

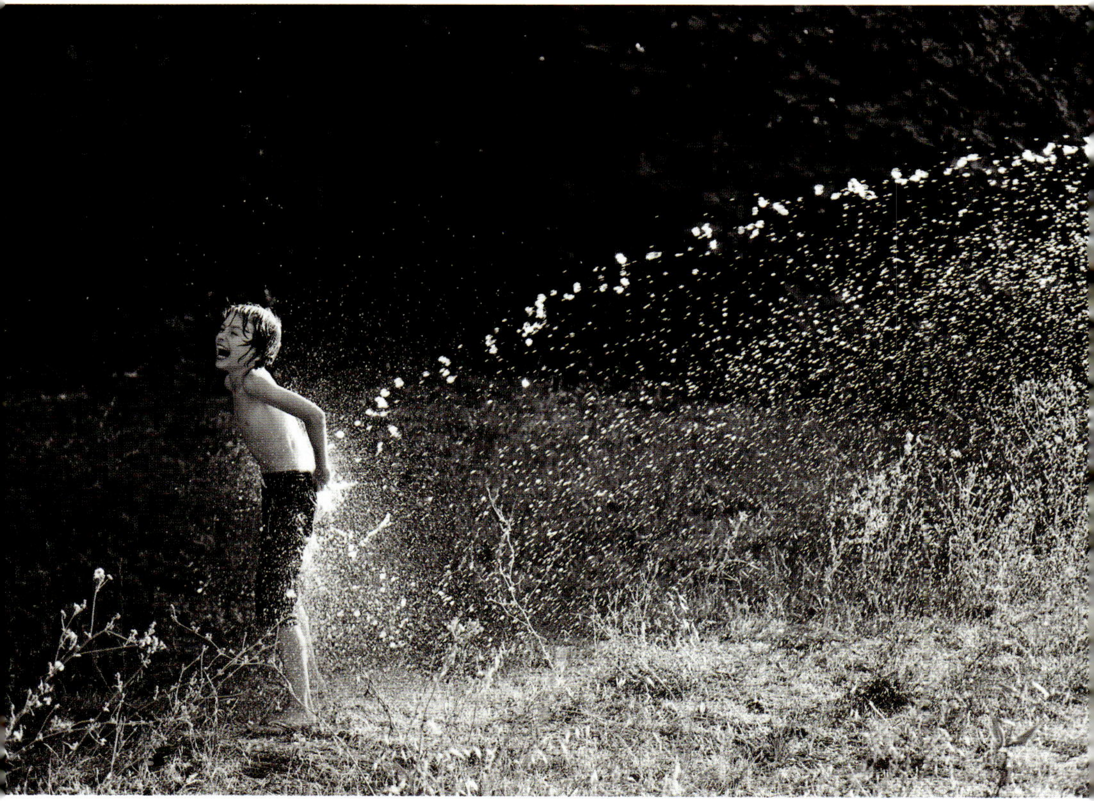

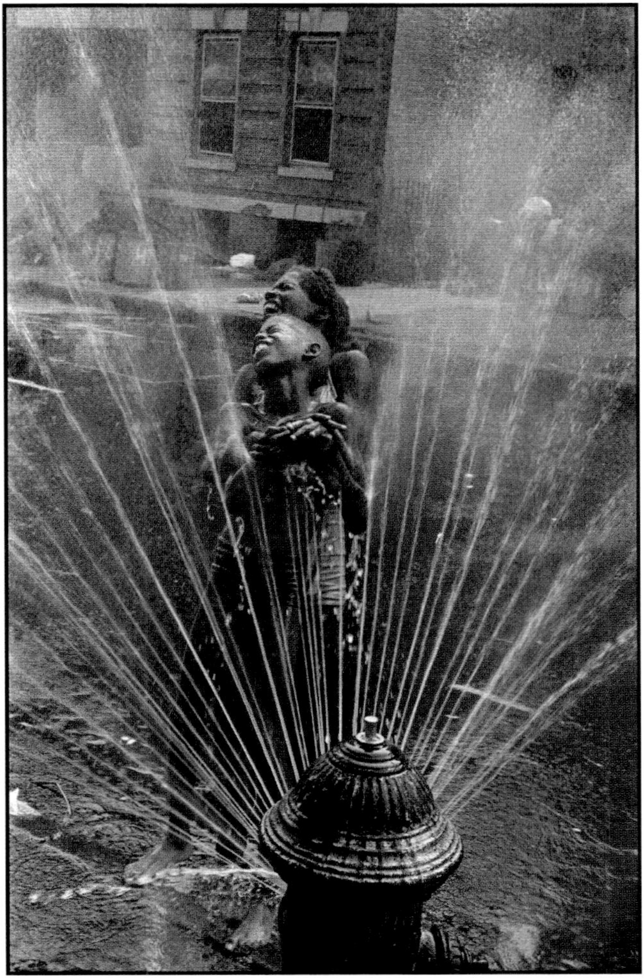

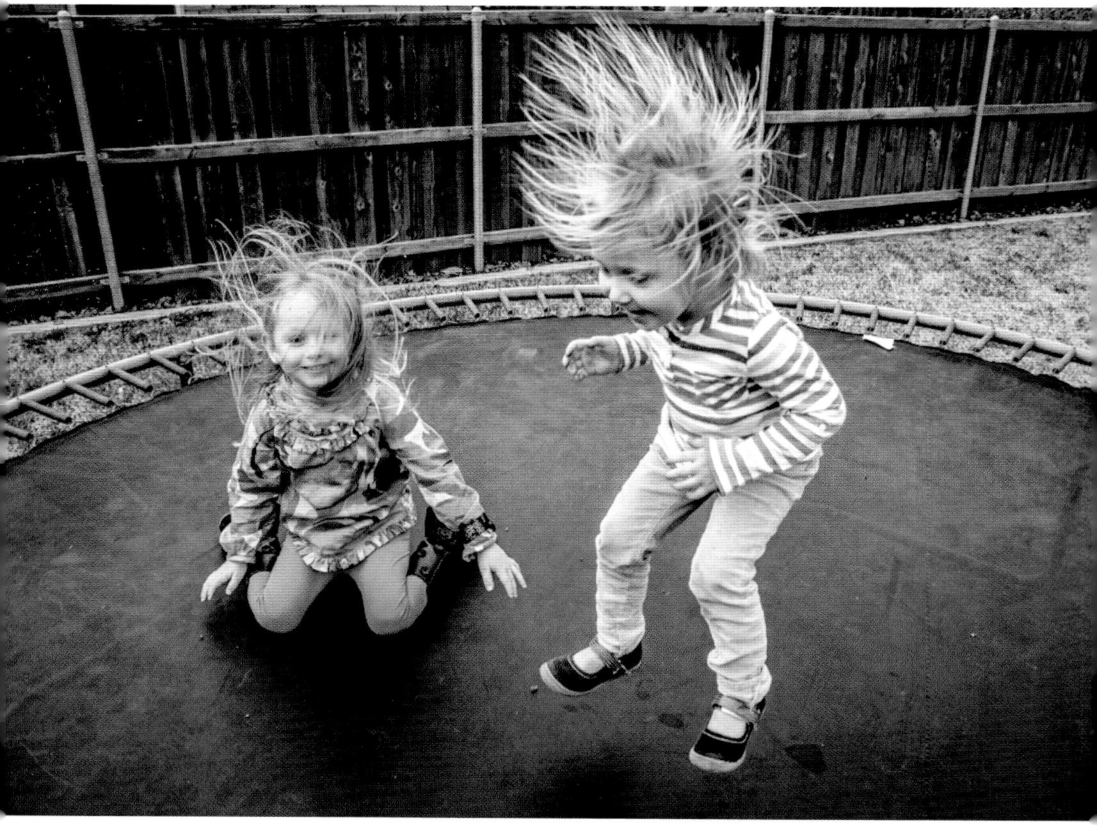

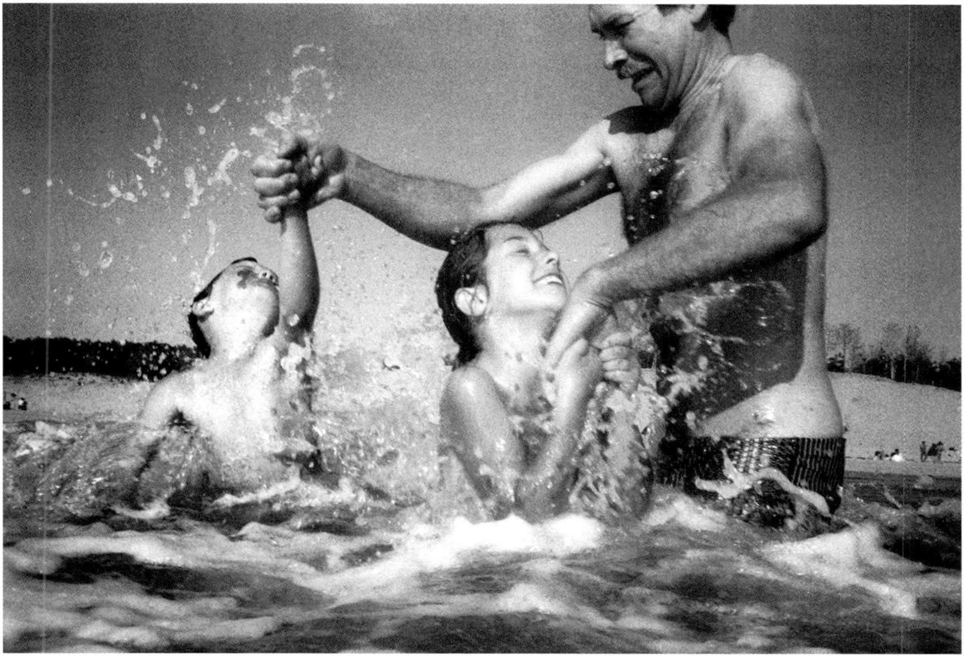

16 17

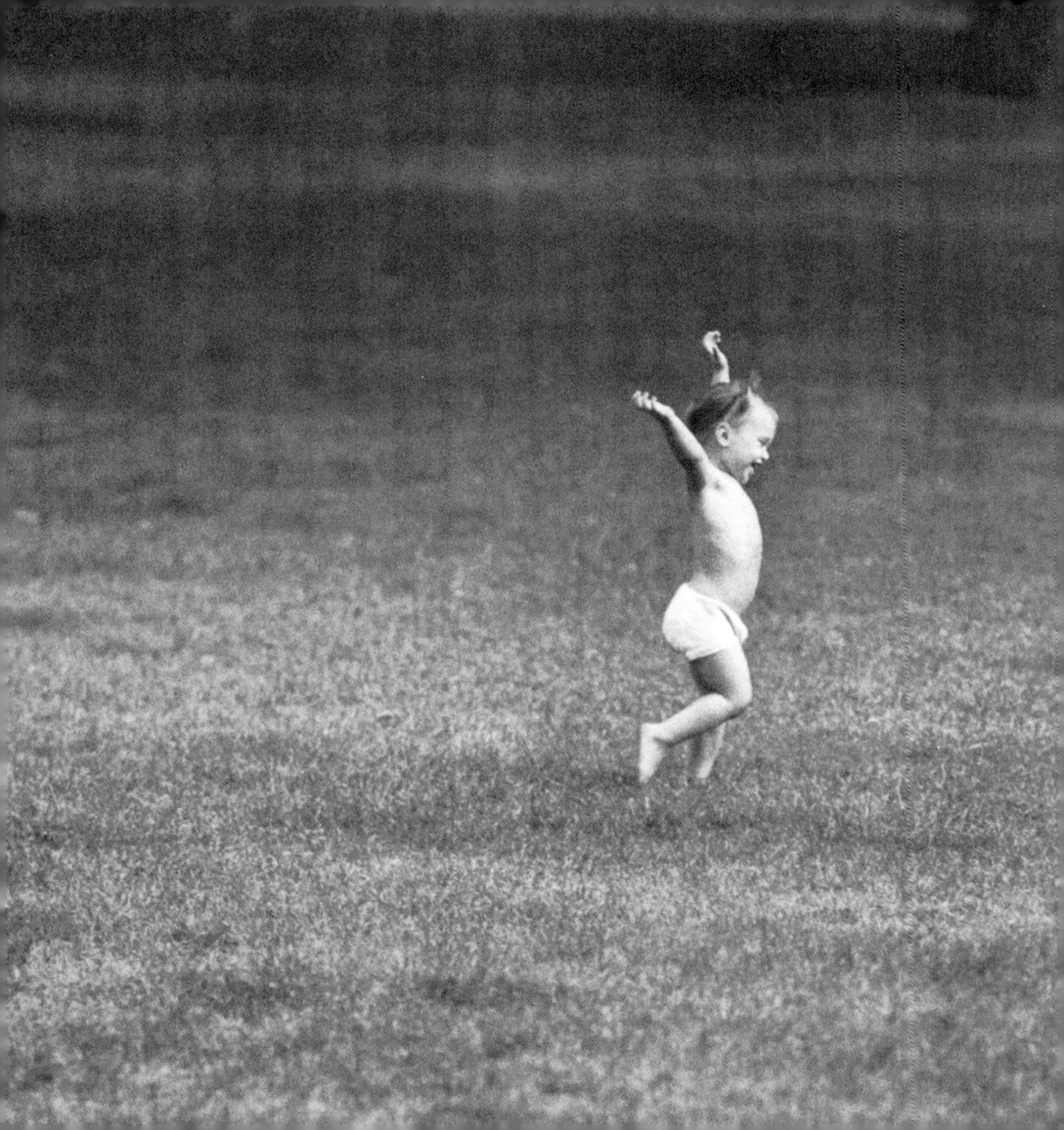

Find ecstasy in life;
the mere sense of living
is joy enough.

EMILY DICKINSON

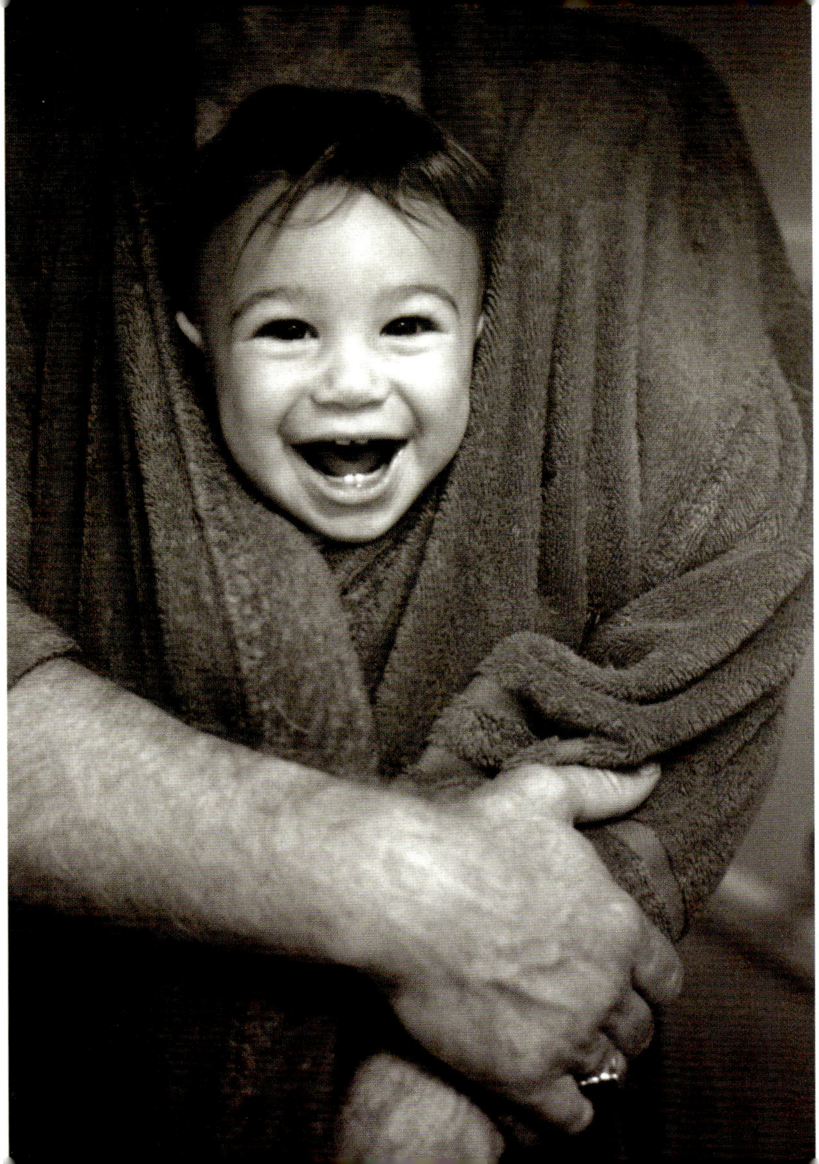

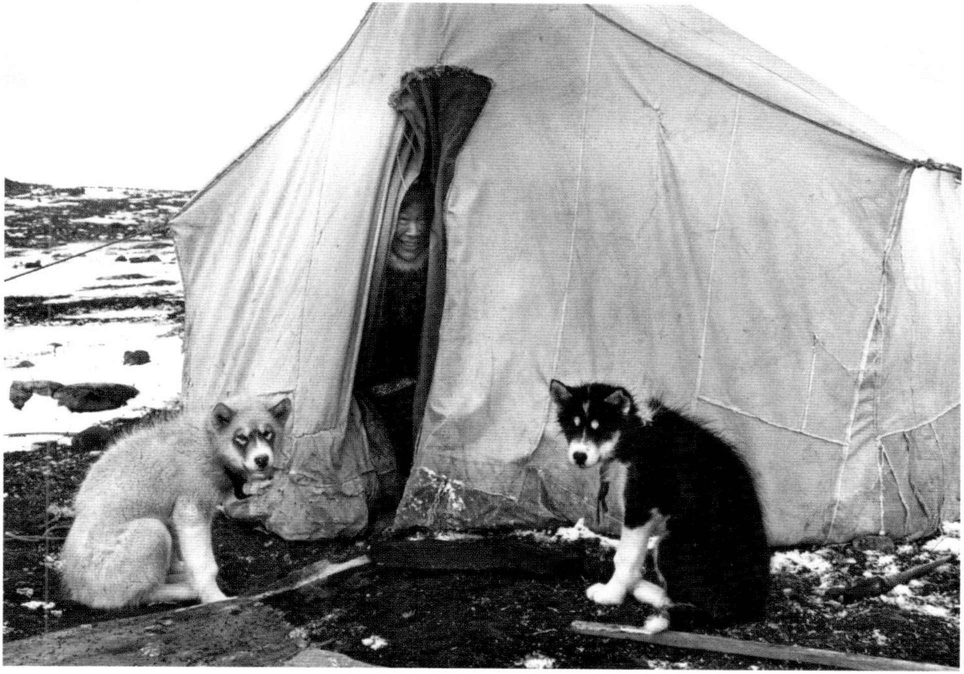

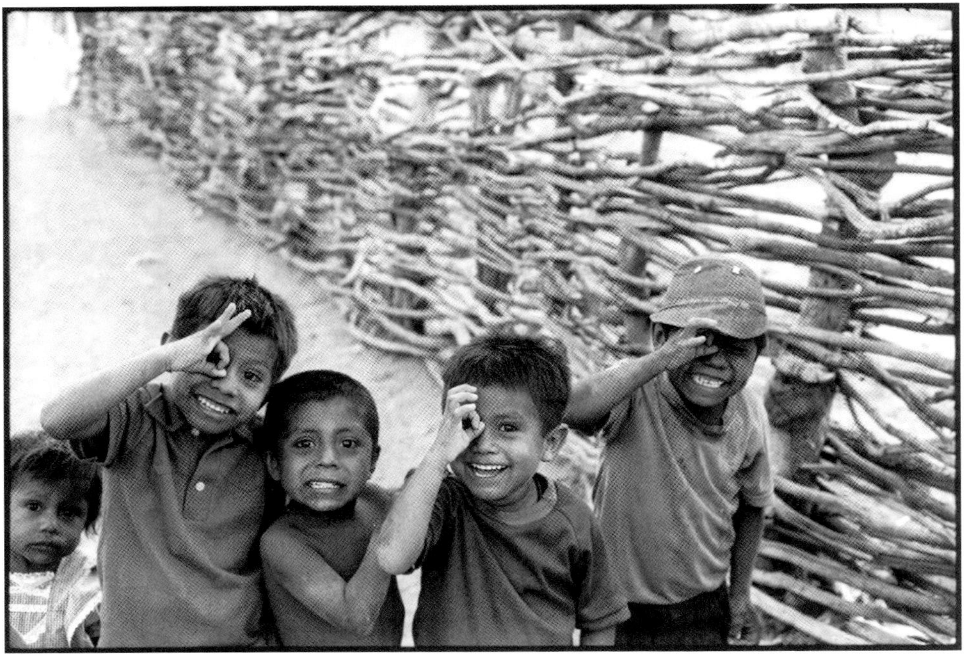

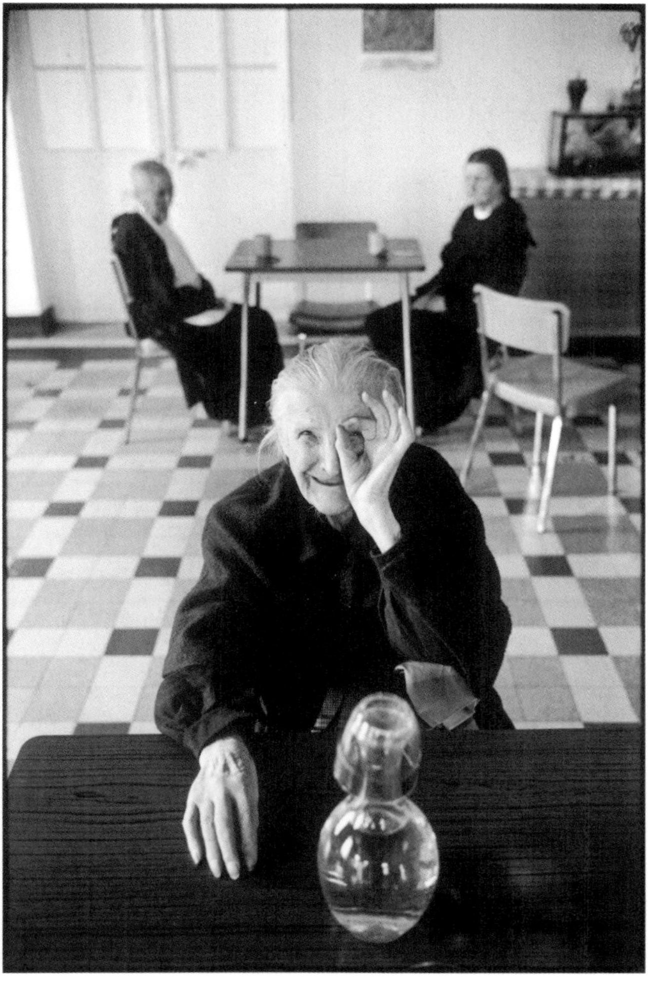

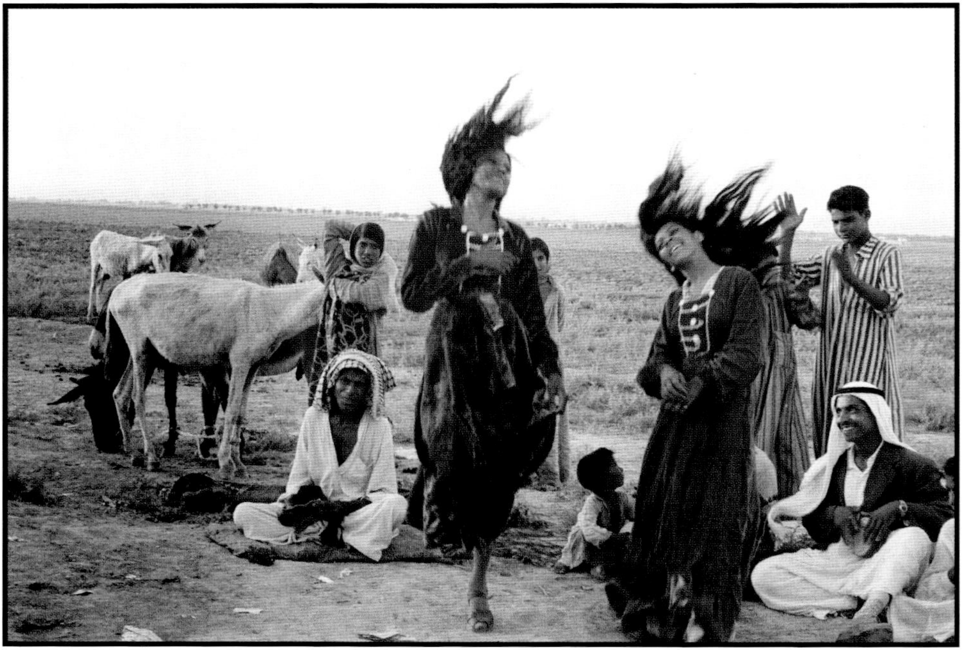

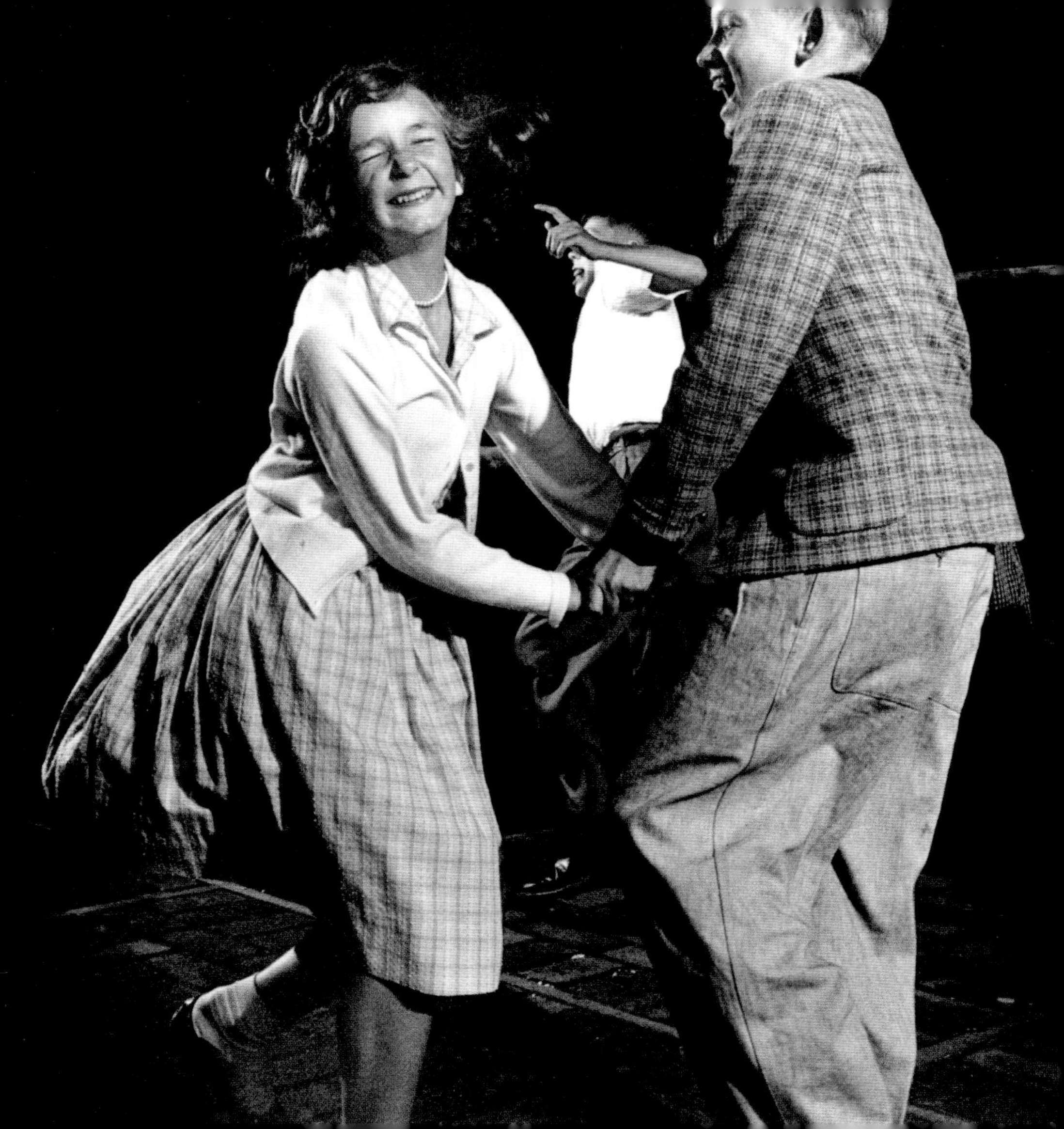

Peace is the beauty of life. It is sunshine. It is the smile of a child, the love of a mother, the joy of a father, the togetherness of a family. It is the advancement of man, the victory of a just cause, the triumph of truth.

MENACHEM BEGIN

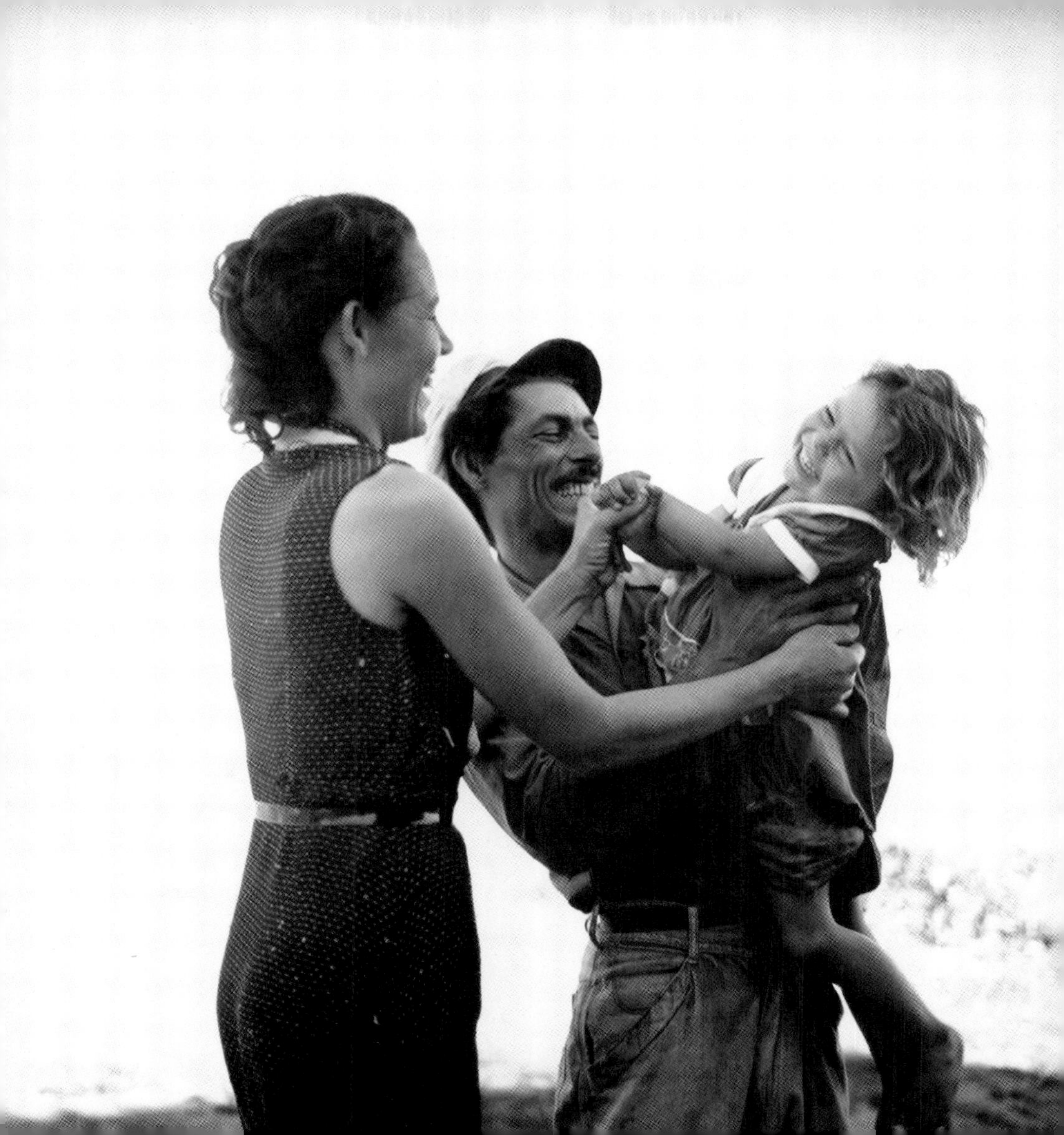

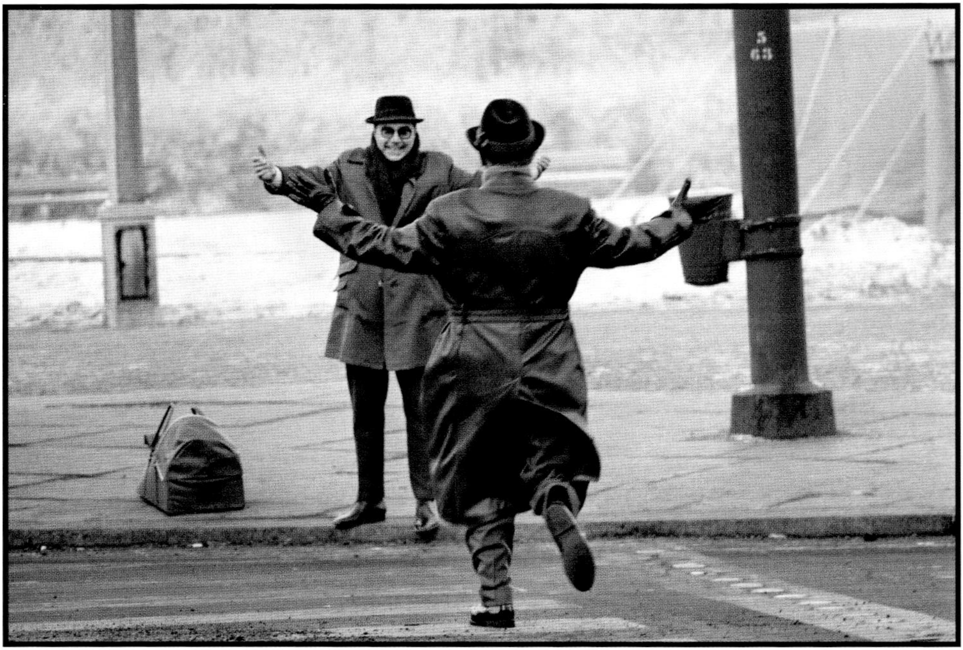
5
63

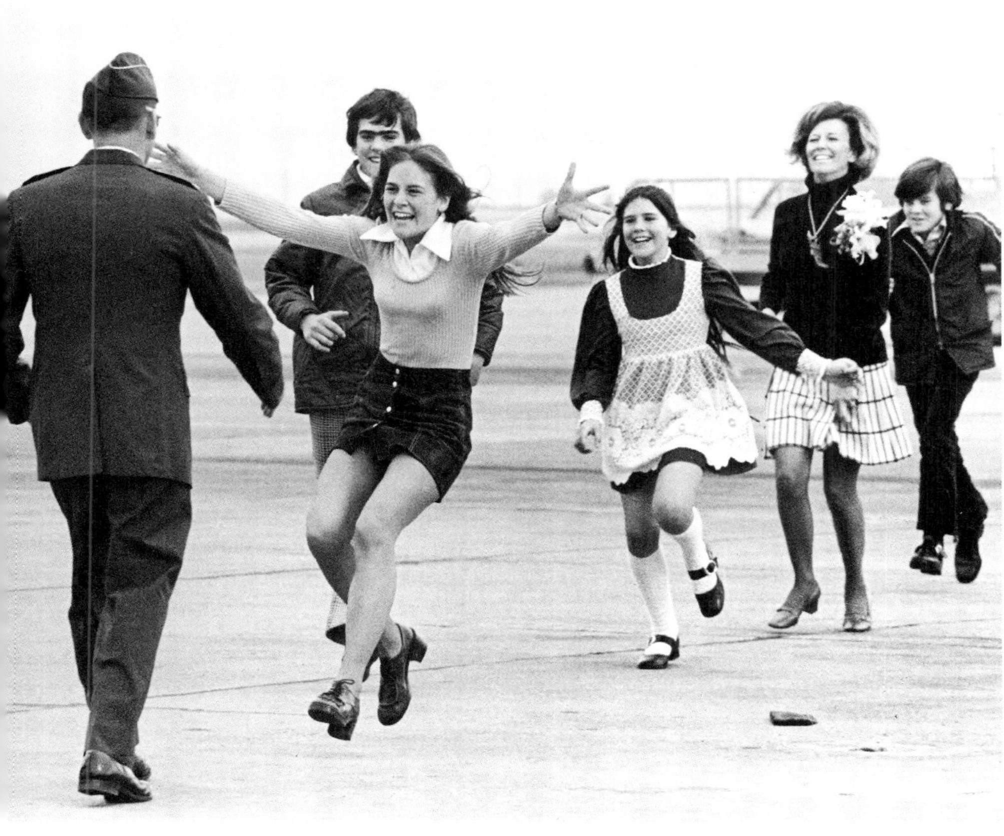

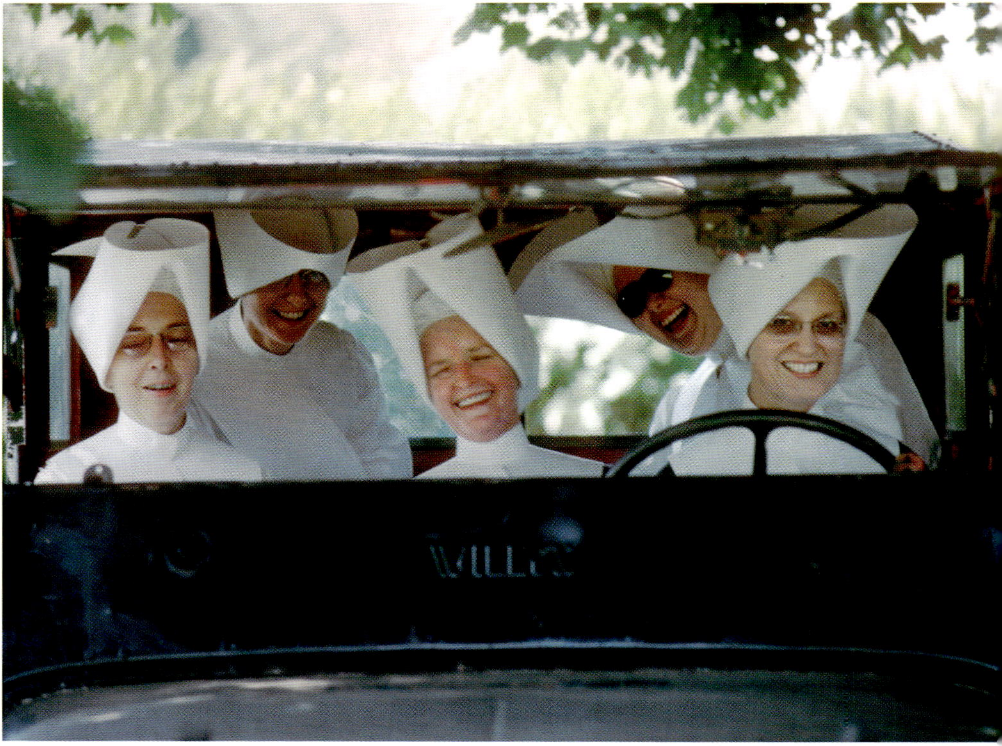

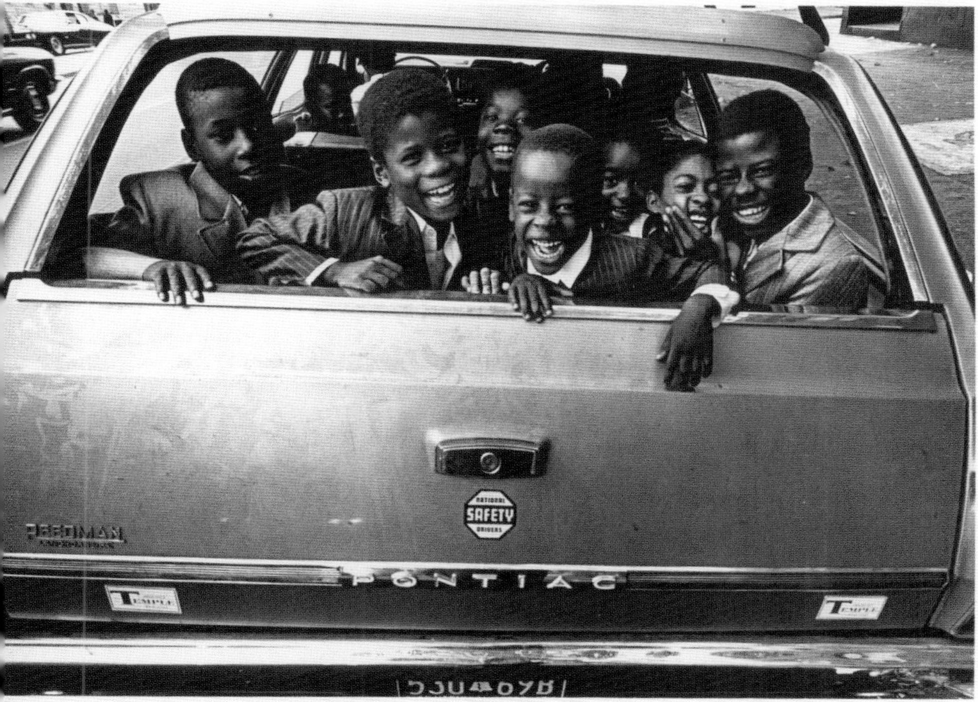
SAFETY
PONTIAC

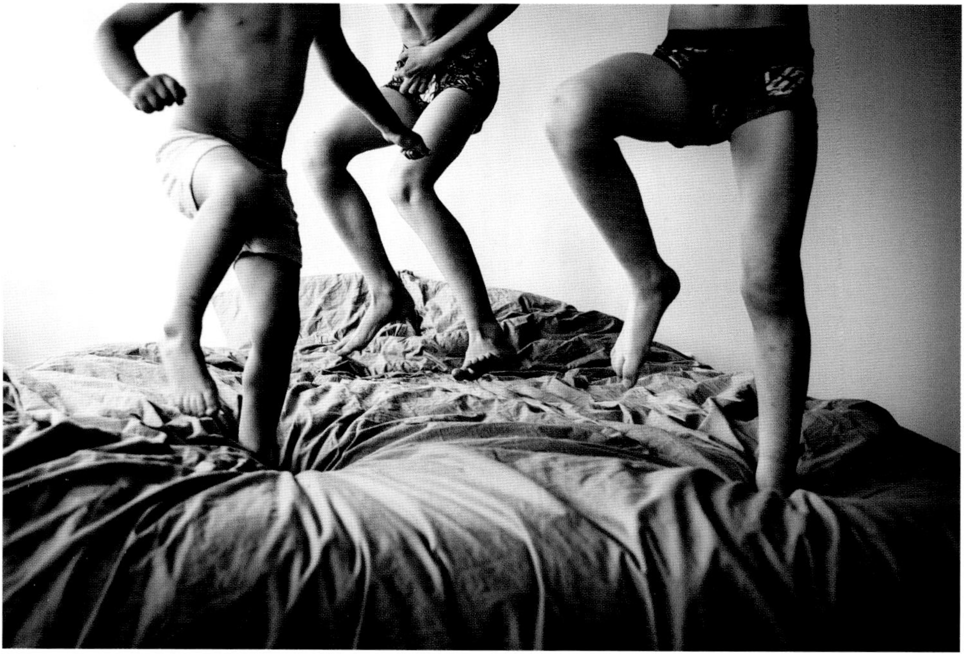

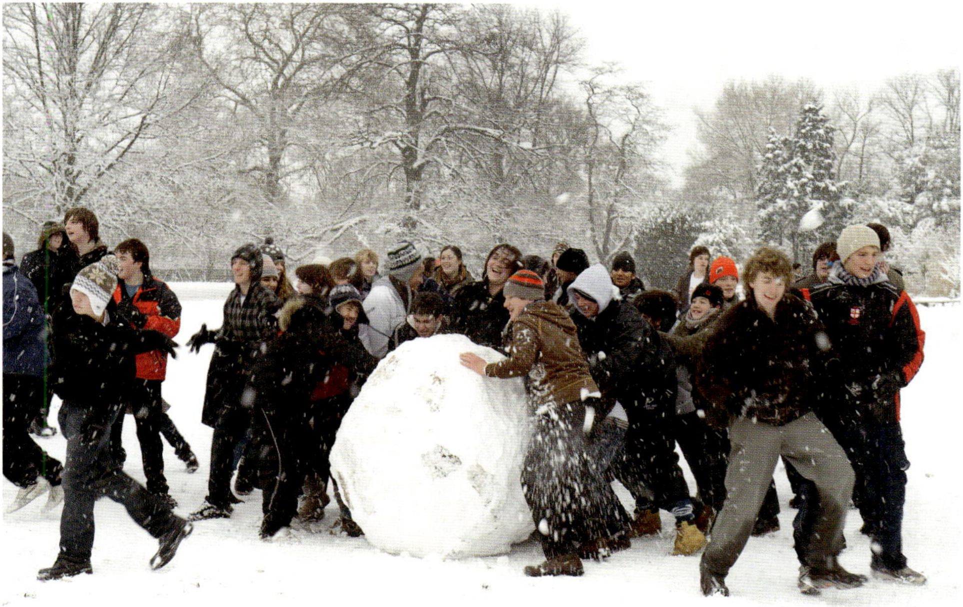

Joy is prayer;
joy is strength;
joy is love;
joy is a net of love
by which you can
catch souls.

MOTHER TERESA

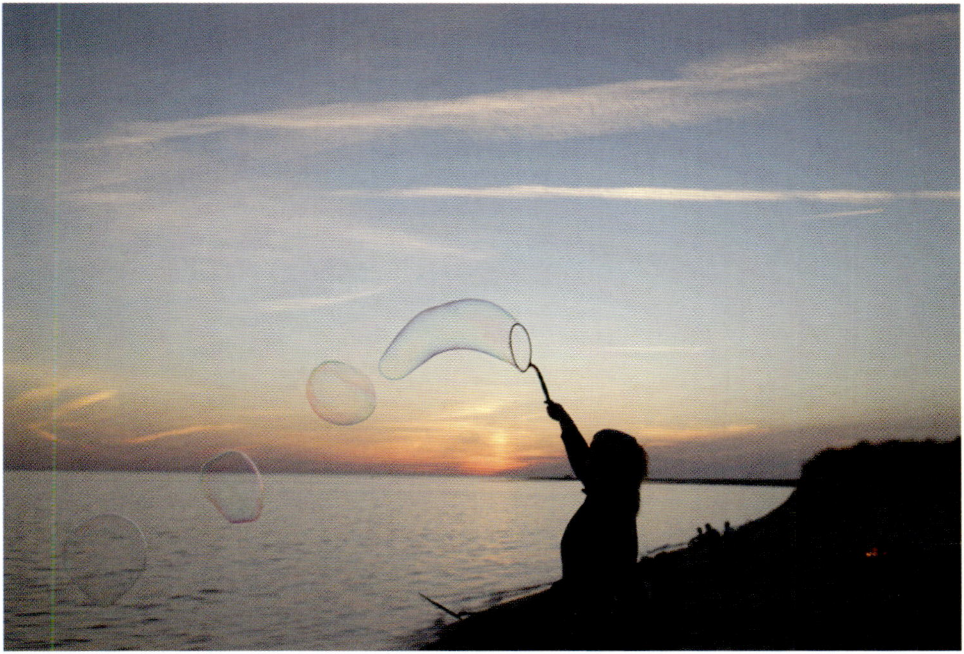

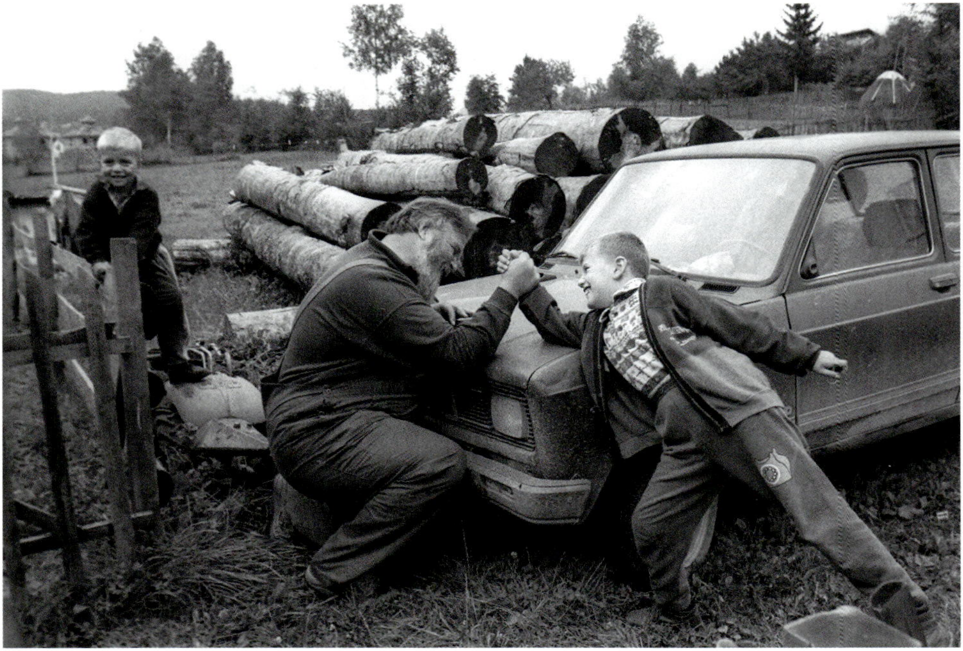

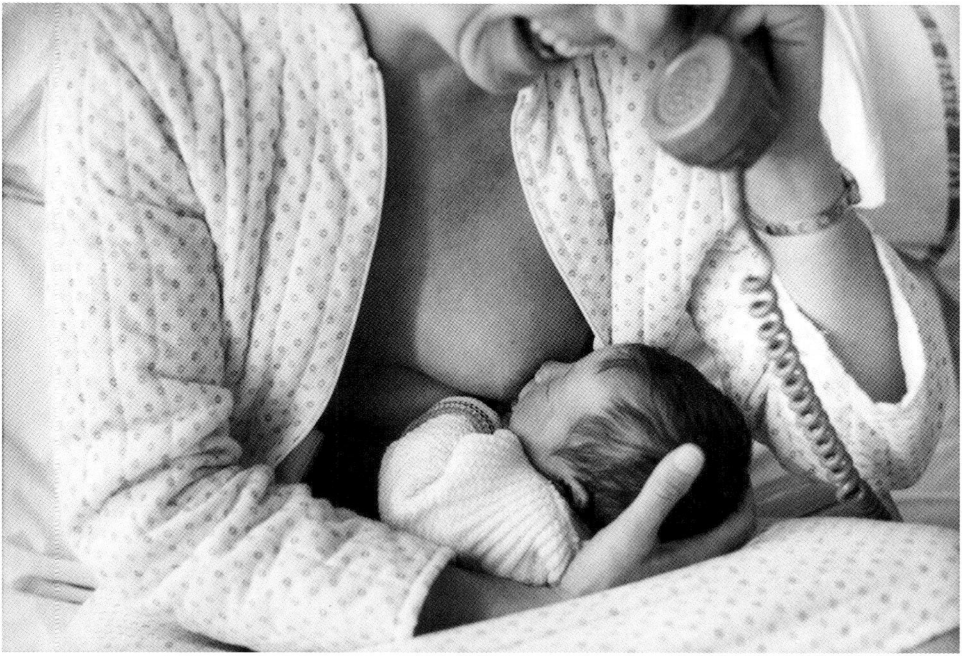

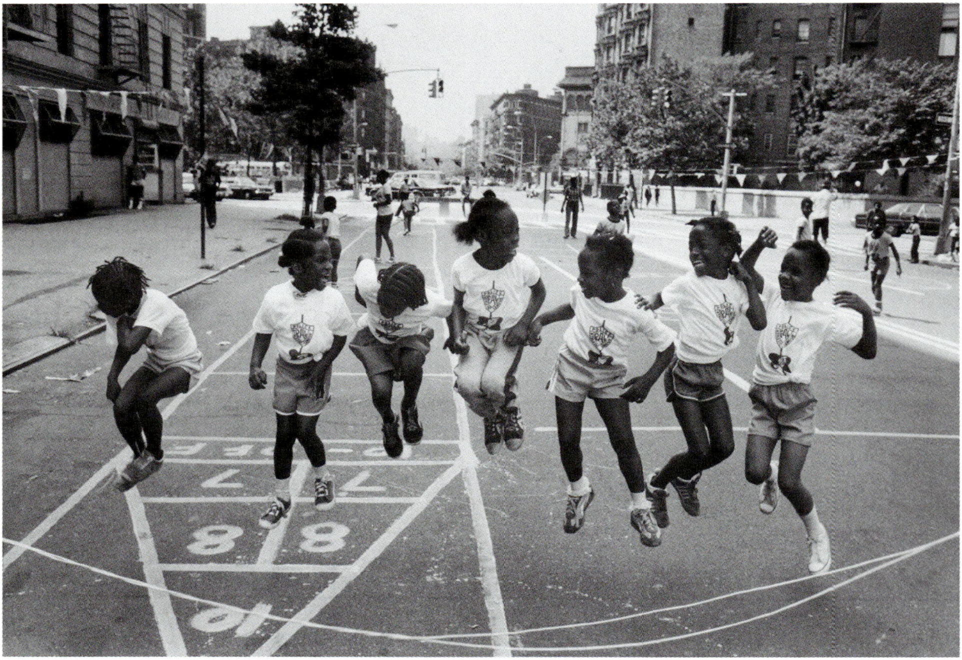

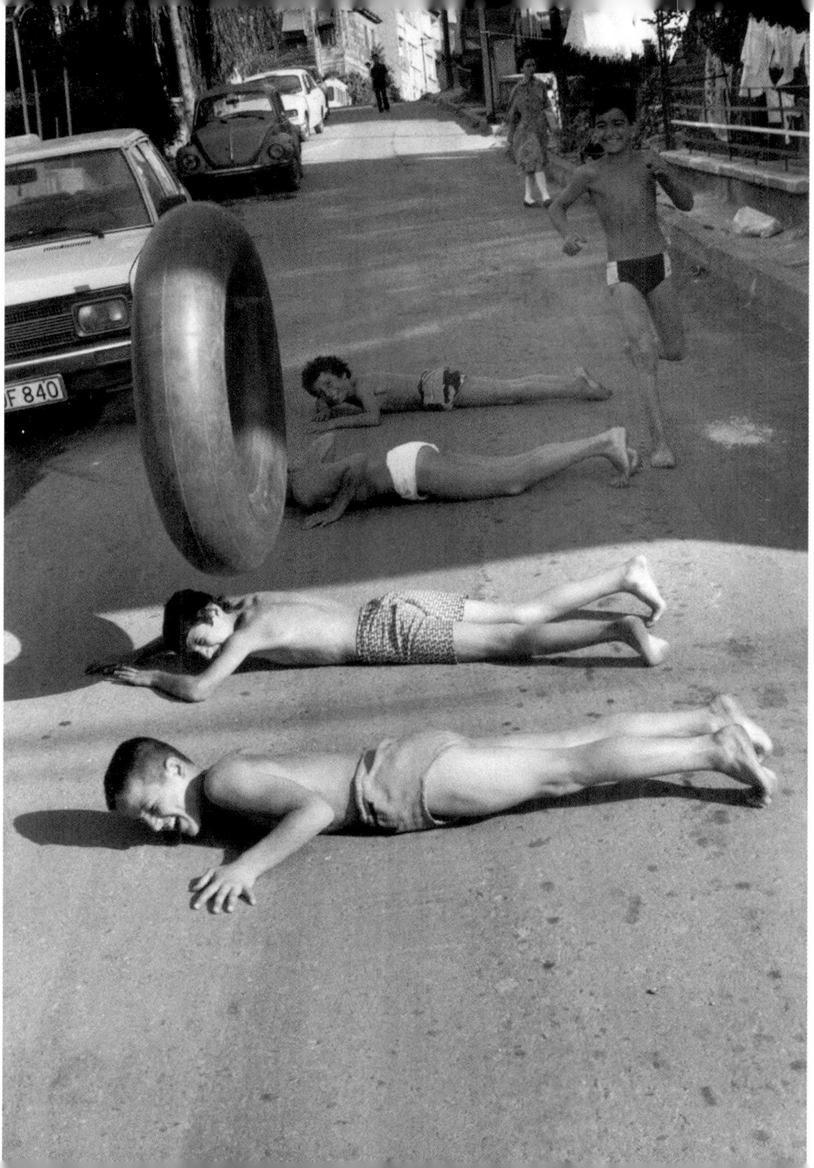

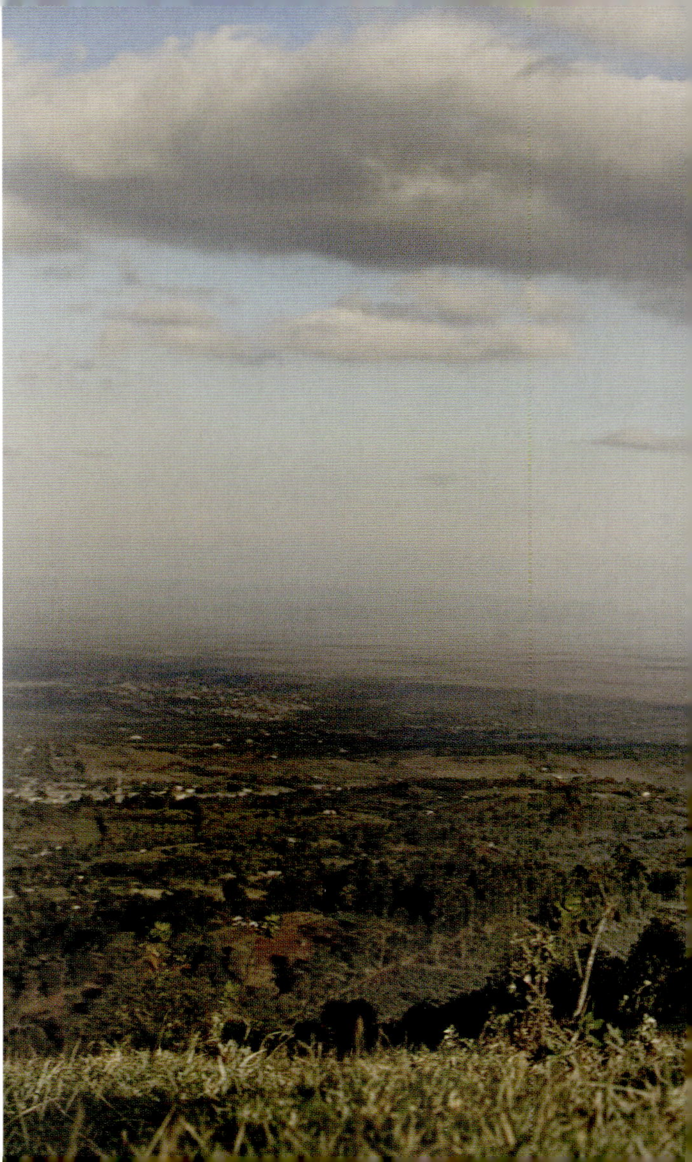

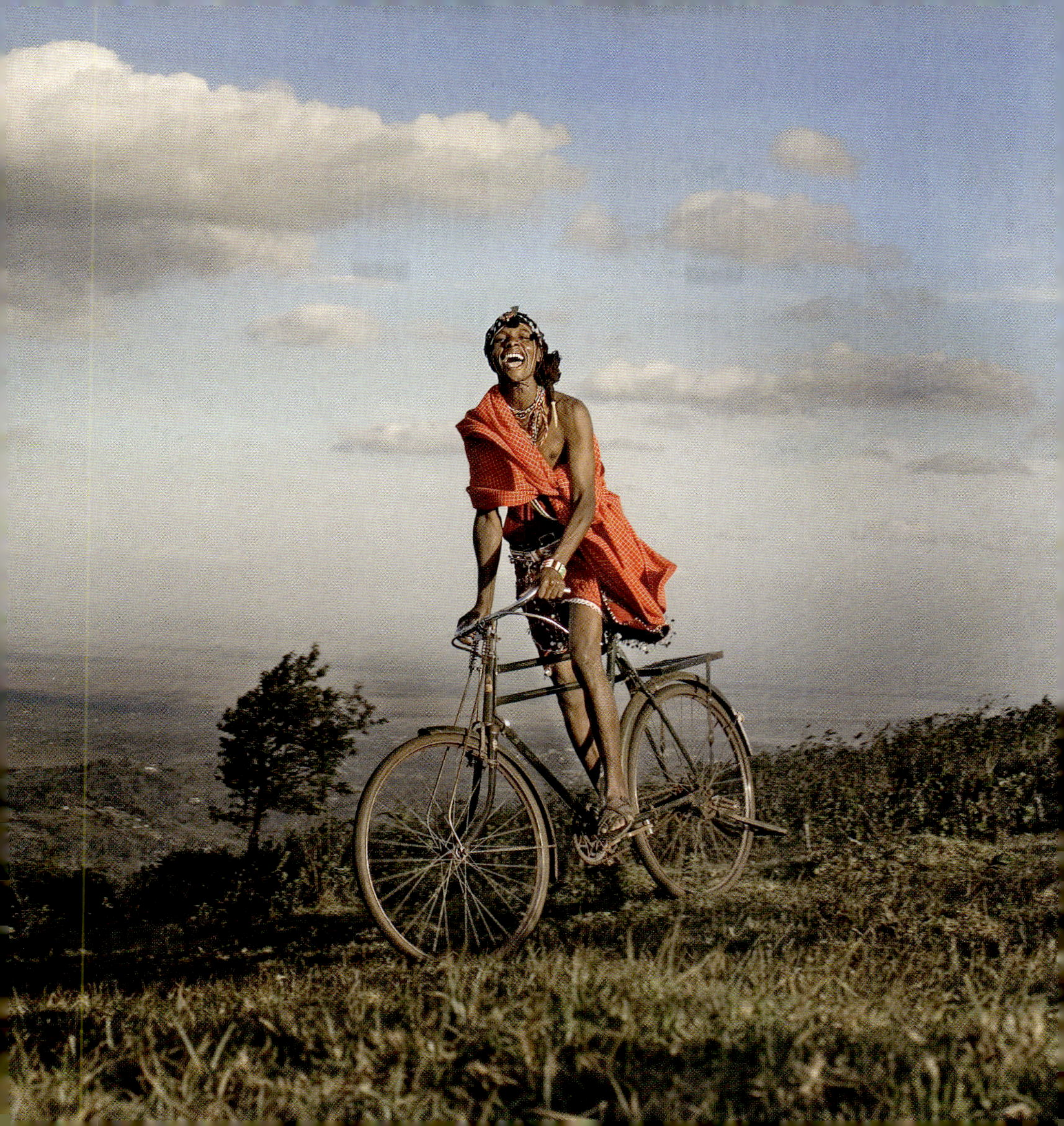

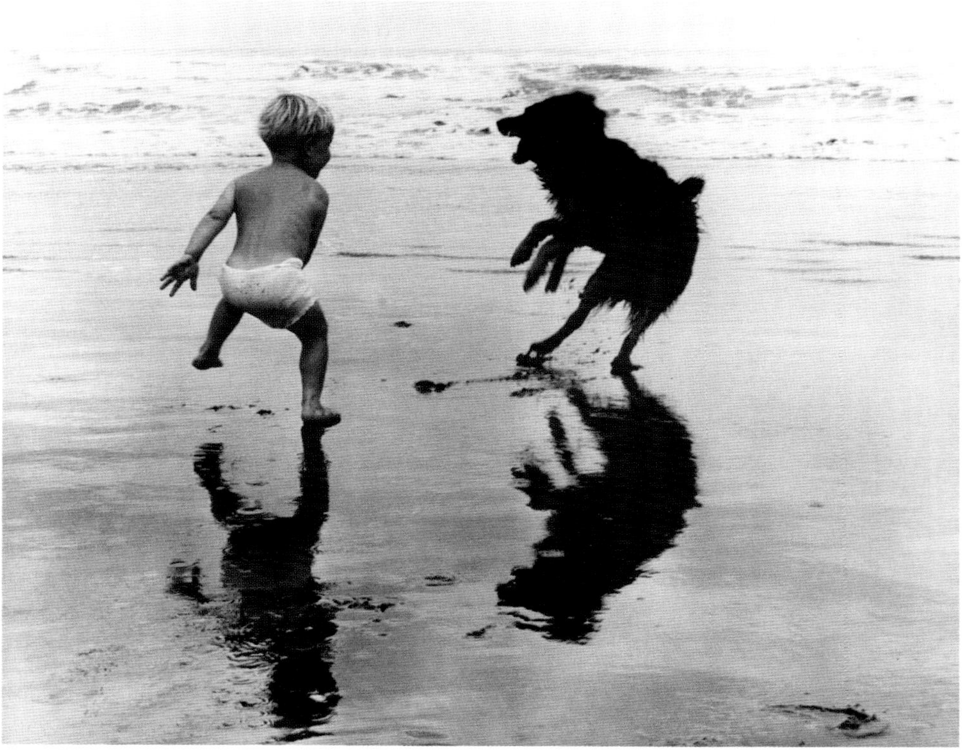

To photograph is to hold one's breath, when all faculties converge to capture fleeting reality. It's at that precise moment that mastering an image becomes a great physical and intellectual joy.

HENRI CARTIER-BRESSON

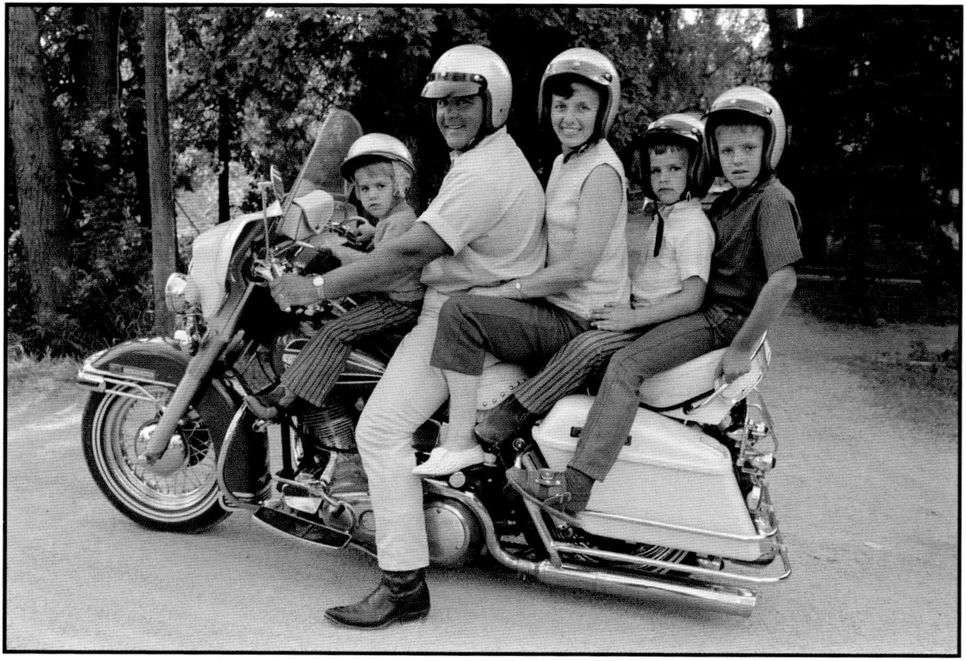

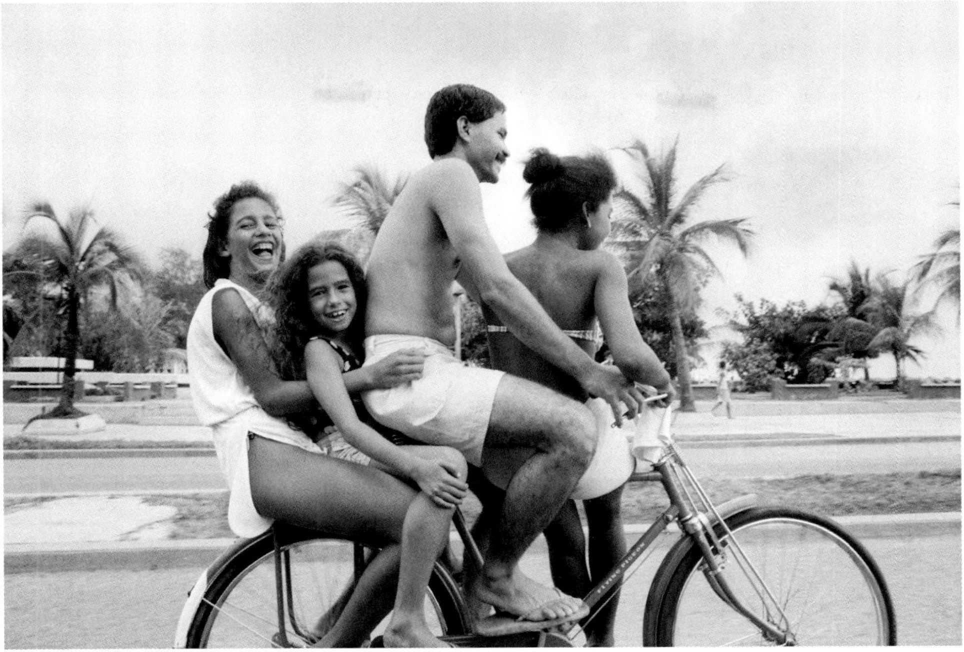

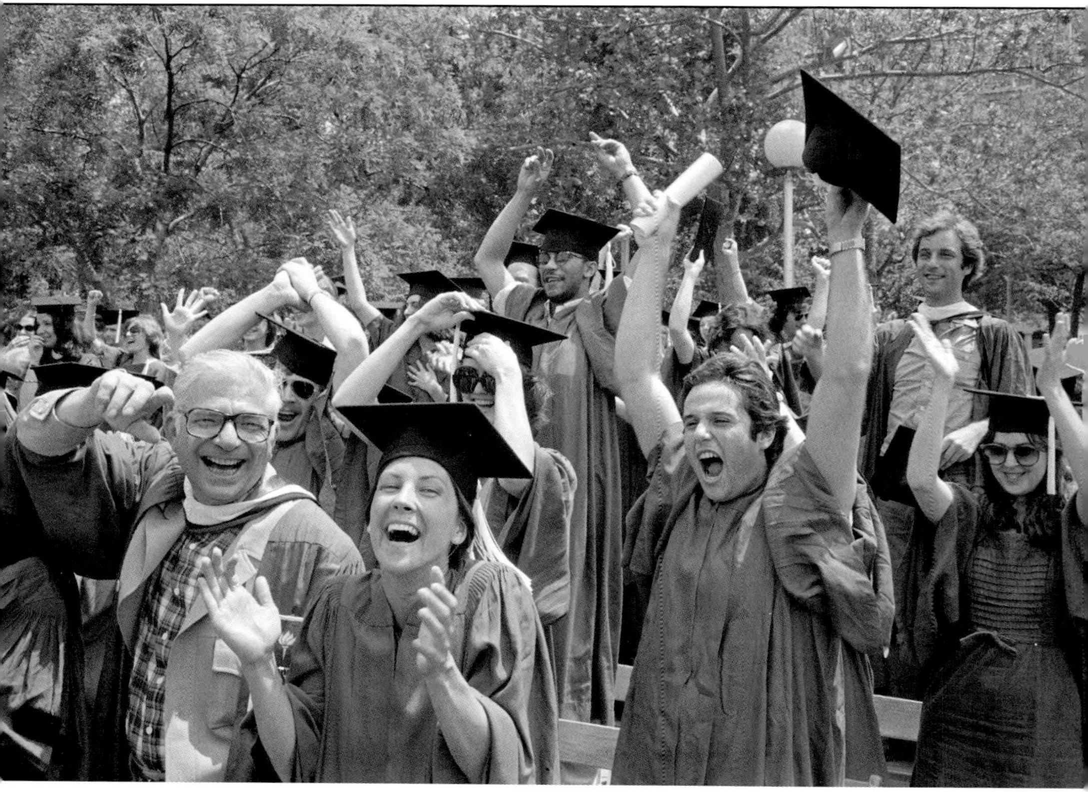

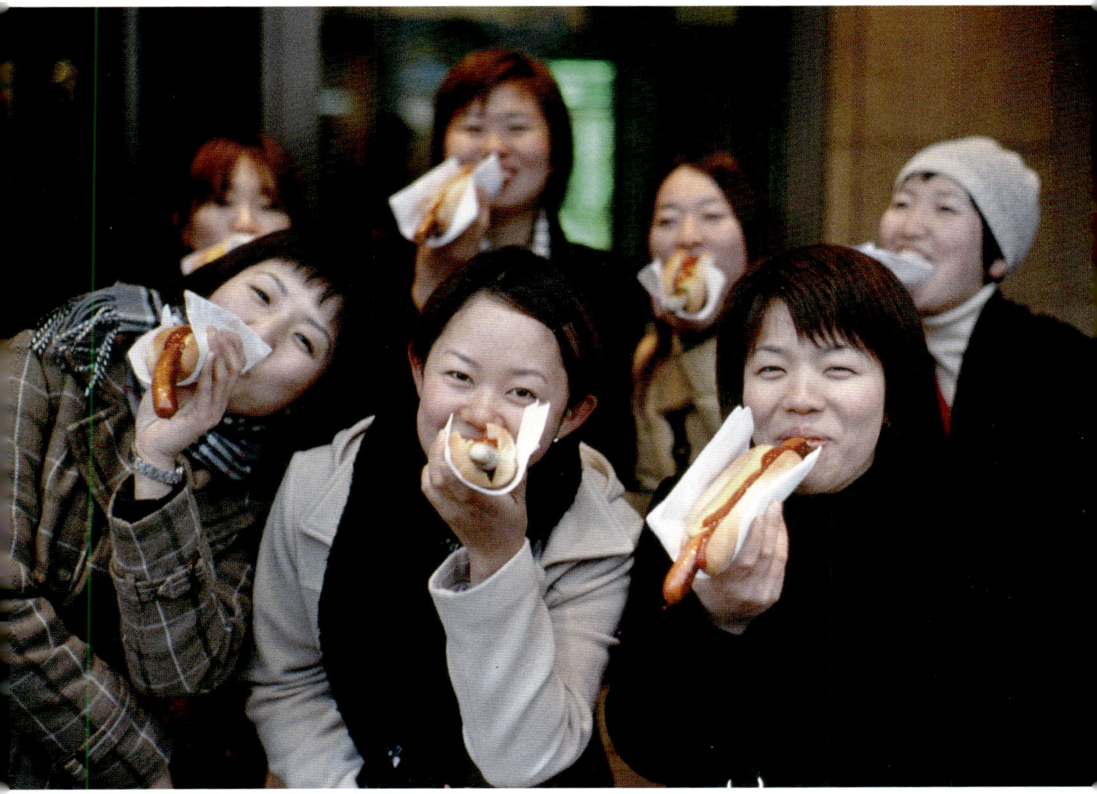

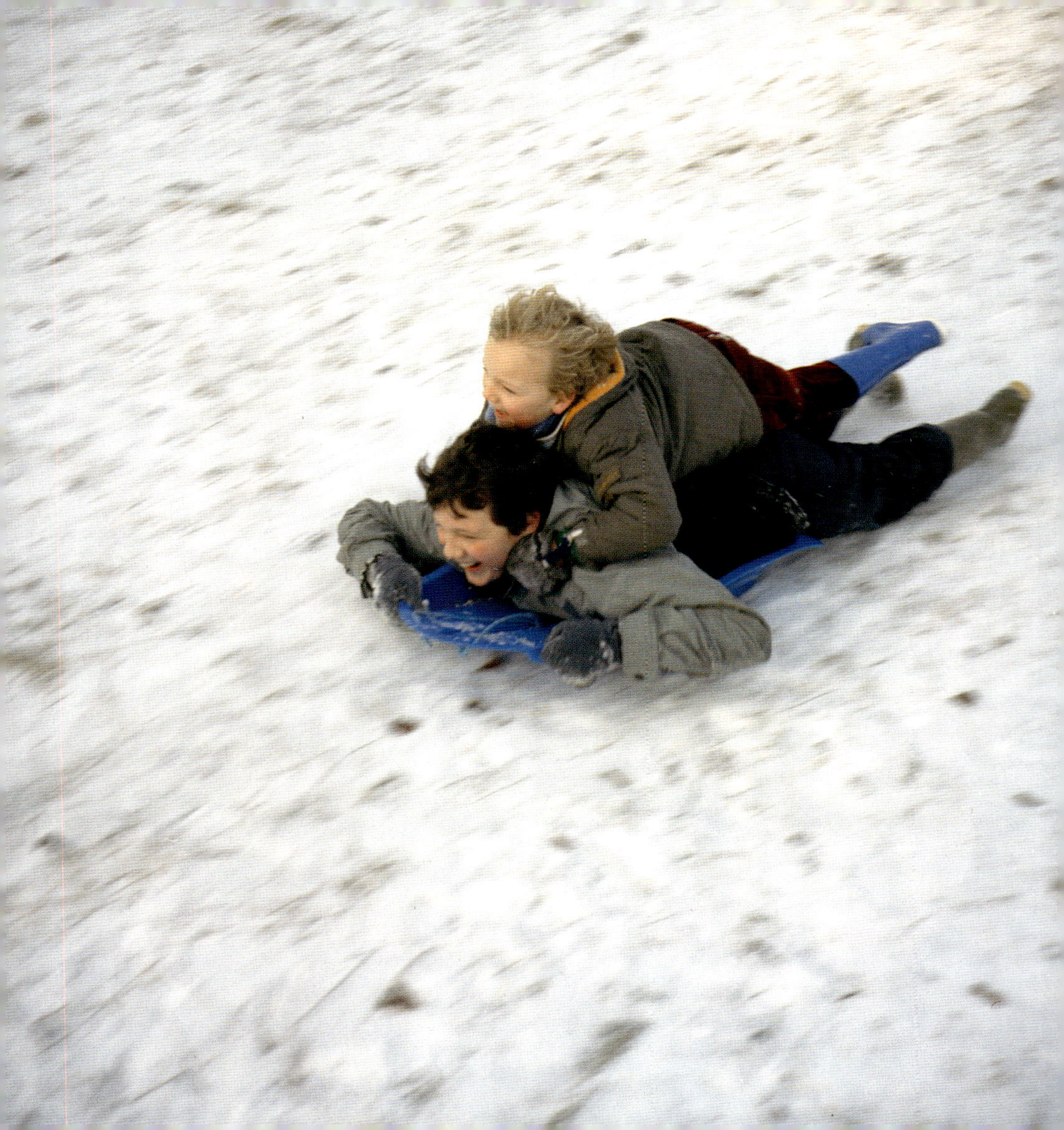

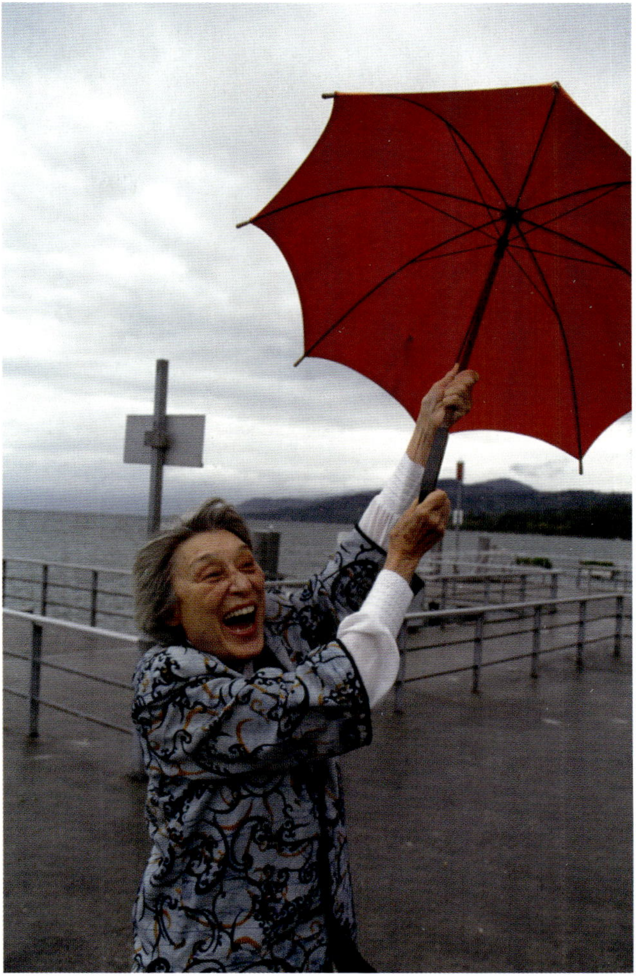

43 44

To get the full value of joy you must have someone to divide it with.

MARK TWAIN

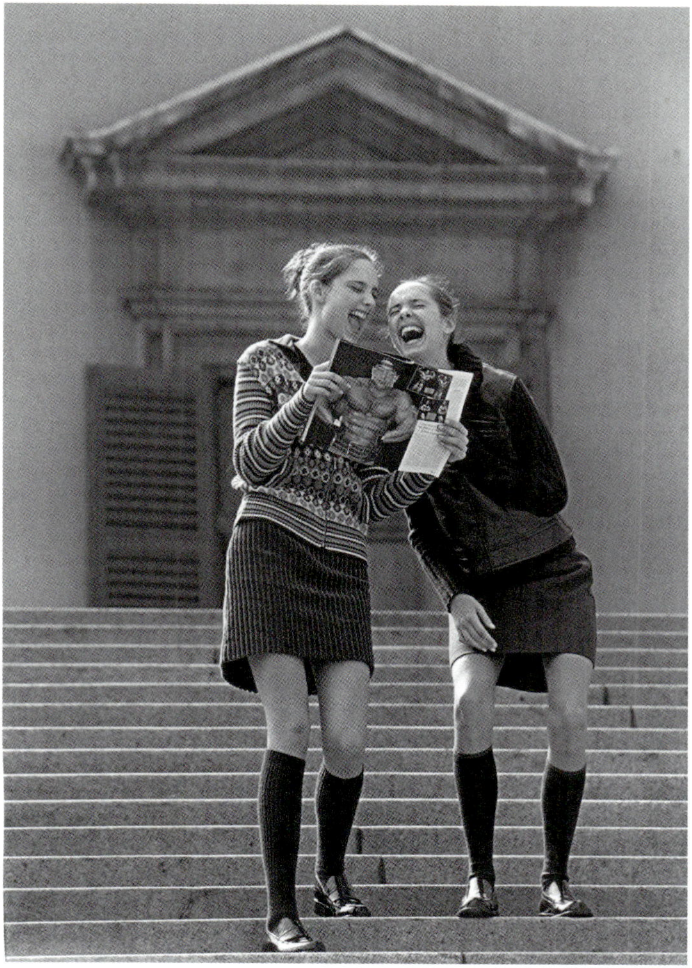

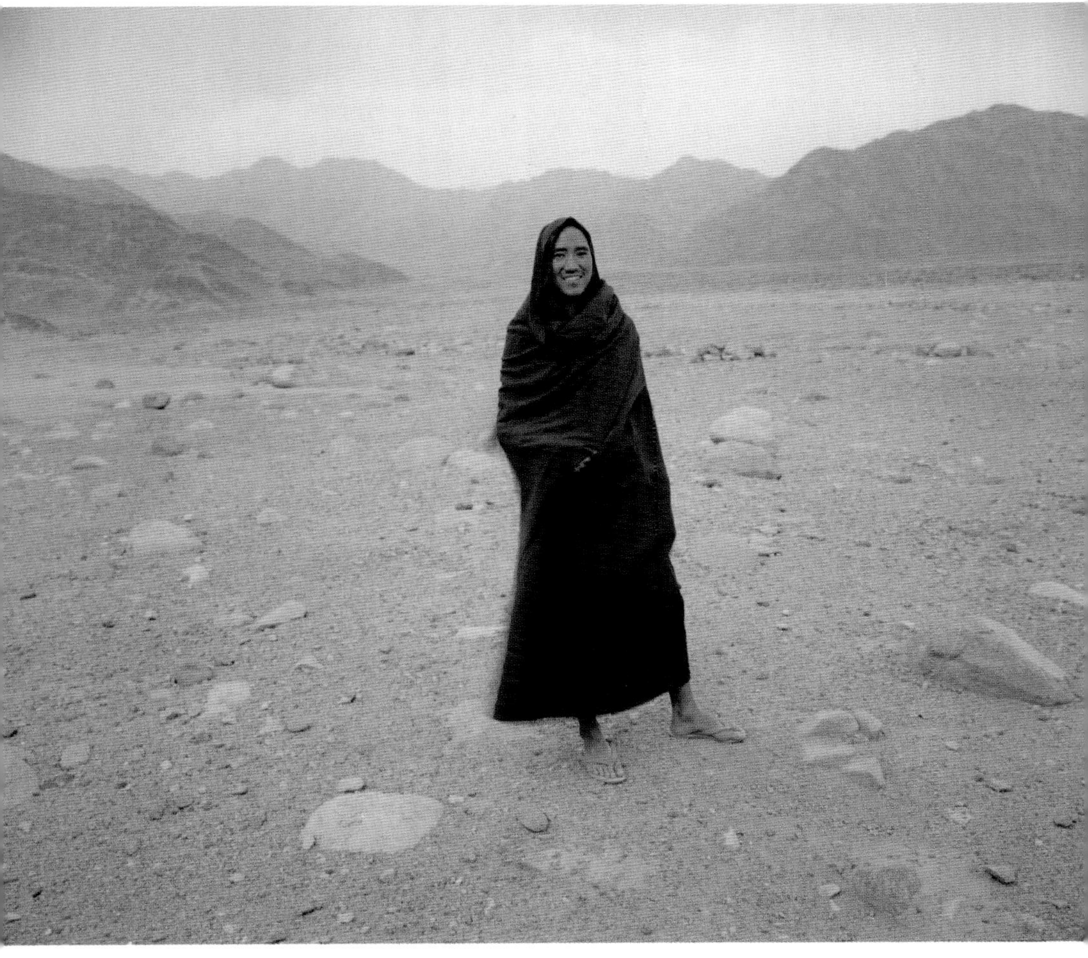

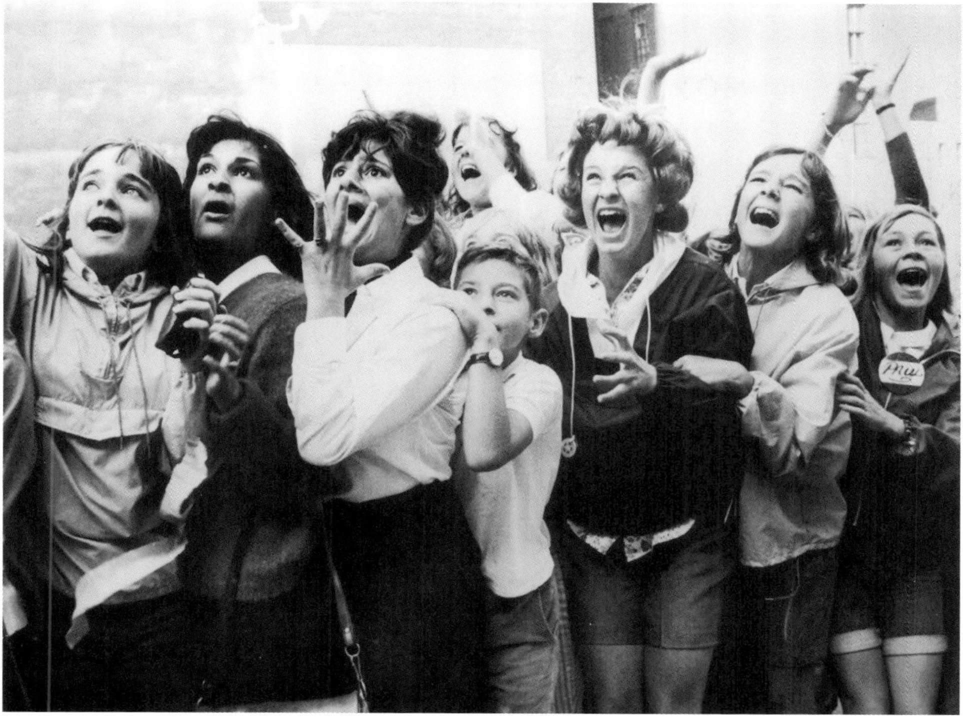

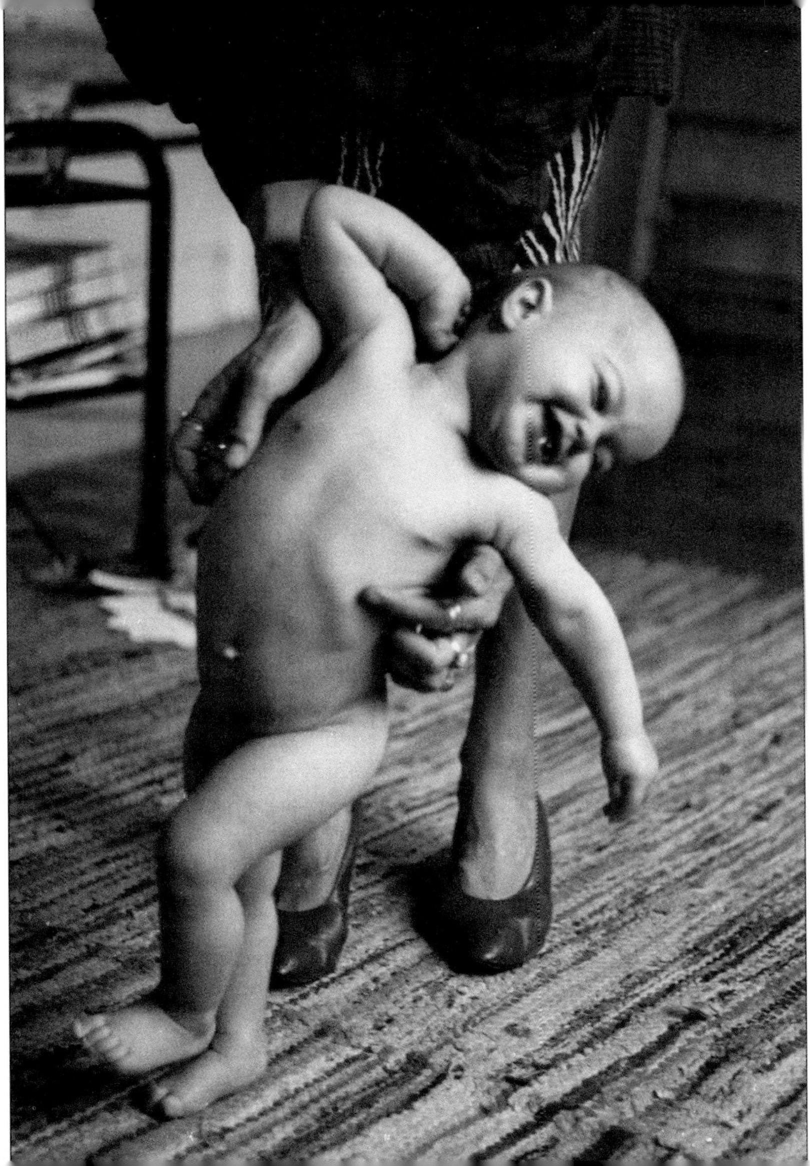

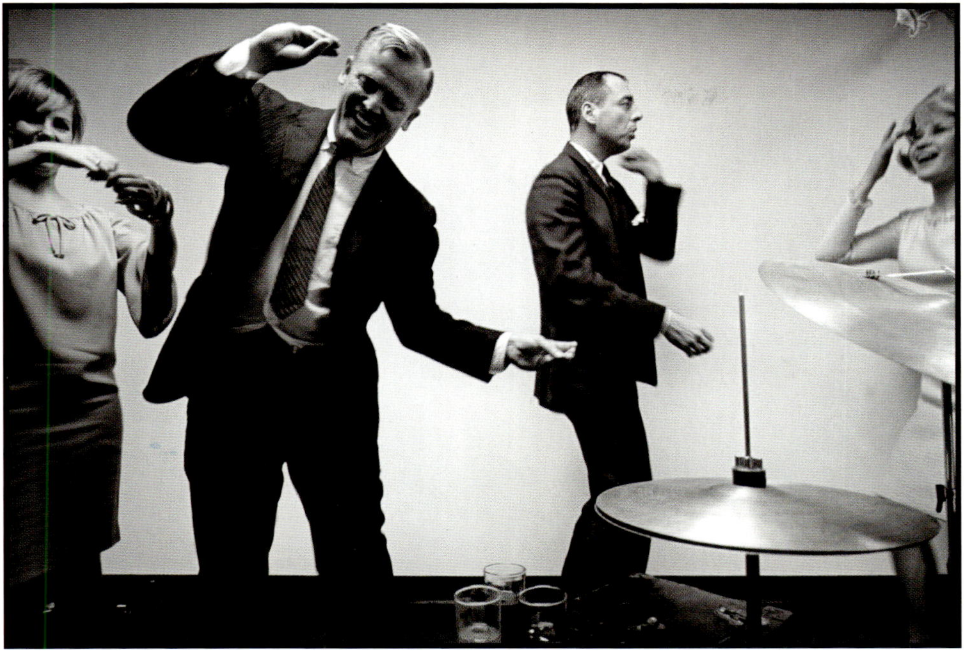

48 49

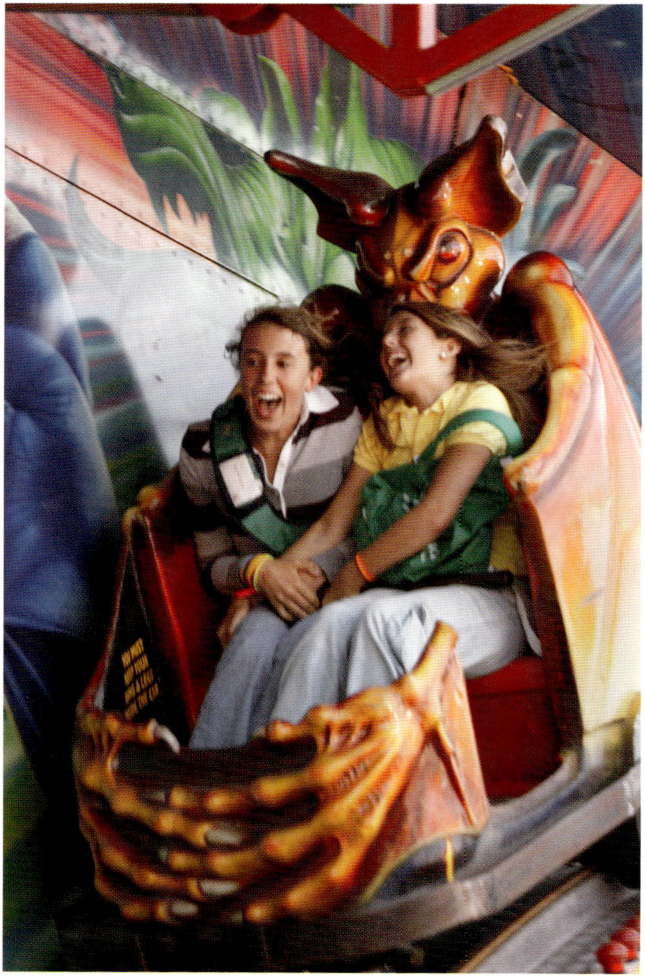

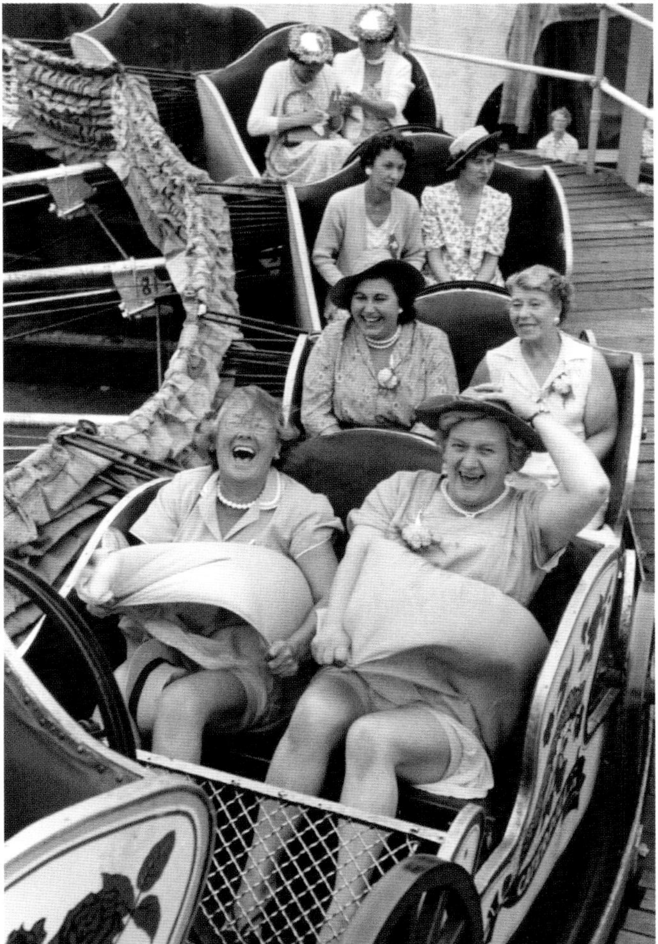

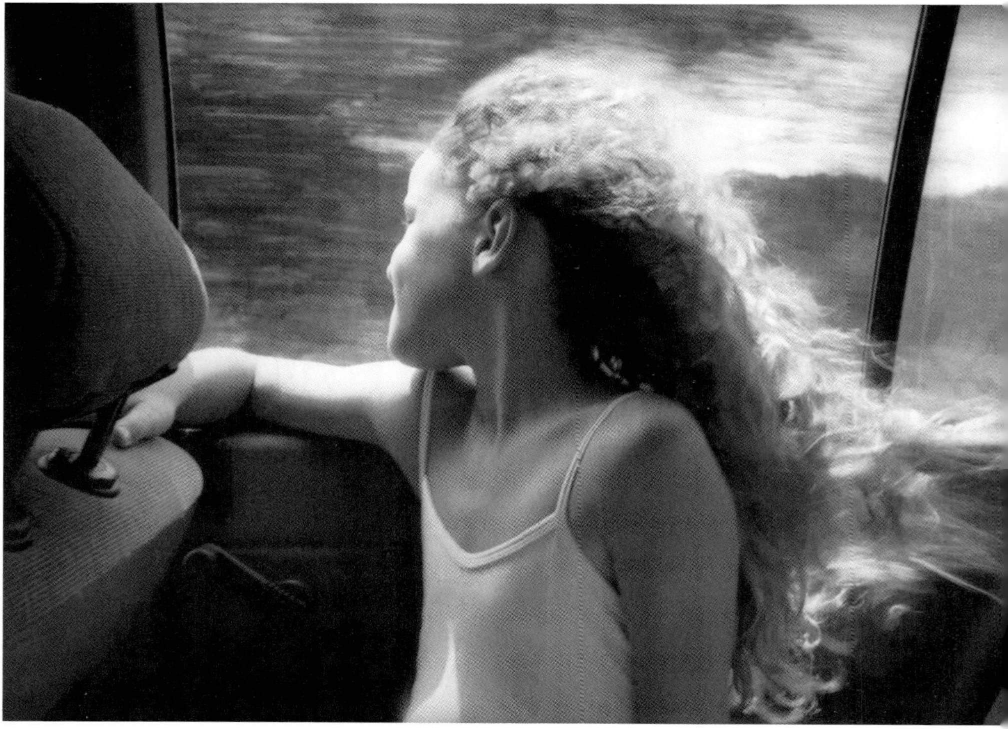

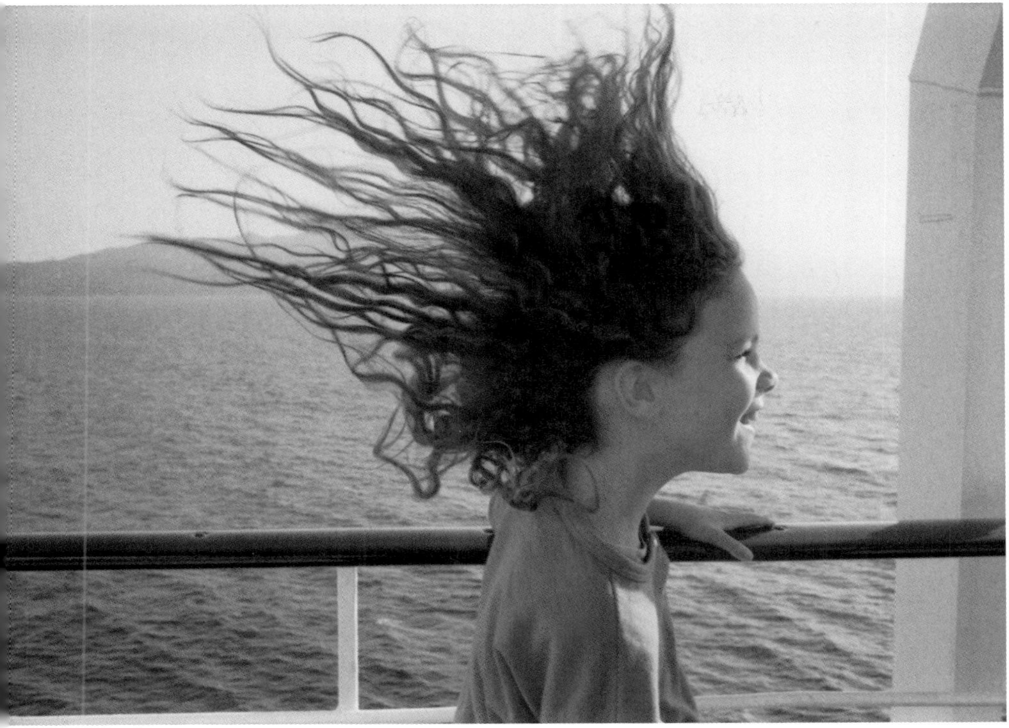

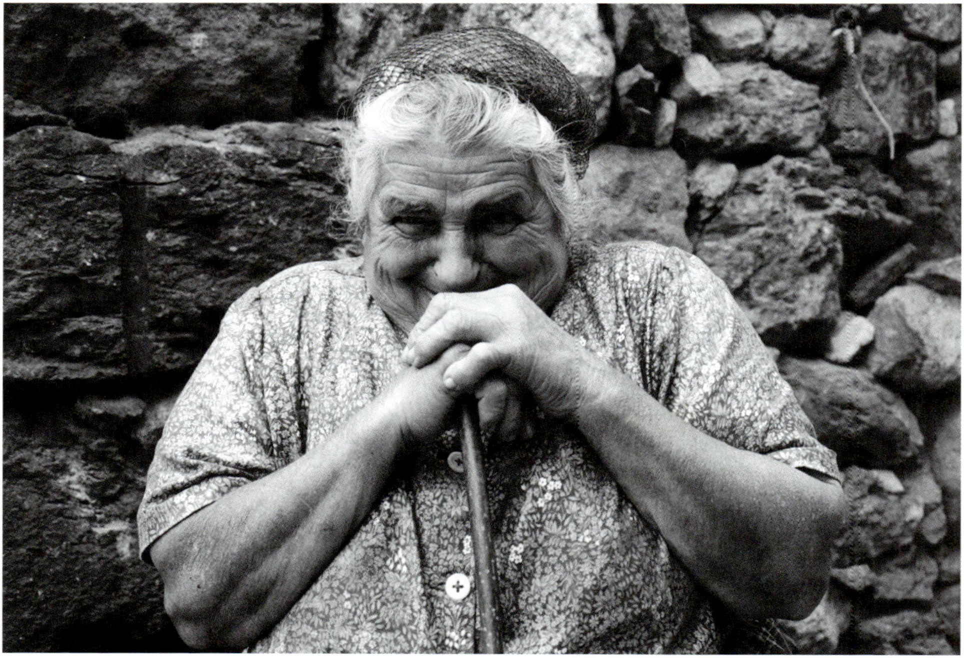

Sometimes your joy is the source of your smile, but sometimes your smile can be the source of your joy.

THICH NHAT HANH

IMAGE CREDITS

1 **France, Paris, Gaston**
Richard Kalvar
1980, © Richard Kalvar/Magnum Photos

2 **Przemyslaw Czerwinski of Poland, 2008 Beijing Olympics**
Michael Christopher Brown
2008, © Michael Christopher Brown/Magnum Photos

3 **Running from the Rain, Capri, Italy**
David Hurn
1964, © David Hurn/Magnum Photos

4 **Wedding, Milan, Italy**
Fernando Scianna
1994, © Fernando Scianna/Magnum Photos

5 **Blanket Toss**
Harold Feinstein
1955, © Harold Feinstein Photography Trust/Getty Images

6 **Backyard Olympics**
Art Shay
1958, © Art Shay

7 **Joy**
Tytia Habing
2014, © Tytia Habing

8 **Little Girl and Pigeons, Venice, Italy**
Francois Le Diascorn
1980, © Getty Images

9 **Reunited, Cuba, Havana**
Bert Glinn
1959, © Burt Glinn/Magnum Photos

10 **Los Angeles, CA**
Elliot Erwitt
1955, © Elliot Erwitt/Magnum Photos

11 **Group Wedding at the Zoo to Celebrate an Elephant's 80th Birthday, Taiwan**
Chien-Chi Chang
1997, © Chien-Chi Chang/Magnum Photos

12 **President Reagan Laughing at Queen's Remarks**
1983, © Bettmann/Getty Images

13 **Boris Yeltsin and Bill Clinton**
Diana Walker
1995, © Diana Walker/Time Life Pictures/Getty Images

14 **Oh So Fresh**
Lisa Tichané
2013, © Lisa Tichané

15 **USA. Harlem, NY**
Leonard Freed
1963, © Leonard Freed/Magnum Photos

16 **The Backyard Diaries**
Teran Jones
2014, © Teran Jones

17 **Beach of Foncillion**
Jean Gaumy
1982, © Jean Gaumy/Magnum Photos

18 **Untitled**
Ken Heyman
1952, © Ken Heyman

19 **Untitled**
Jenny Gummersall
1991, © Jenny Gummersall

20 **Taloyoak, Nunavut, Canada**
Pamela Harris
1972, © Pamela Harris

21 **Mexico, San Augustin de Oapan Village**
Abbas
1984, © Abbas/Magnum Photos

22 **France, Val de Marne, Ivry-sur-Seine, Hospice**
Martine Franck
1975, © Martine Franck, Magnum Photos

23 **Dancing Gypsies, Iraq**
Inge Morath
1956, © The Inge Morath Foundation

24 **Untitled**
Wayne Miller
1958, © Wayne Miller/Magnum Photos

25 **Cuban Fisherman and Family**
Eve Arnold
1954, © Eve Arnold/Magnum Photos

26 **West Germany, Christmas in Berlin**
Ian Berry
1963, © Ian Berry/Magnum Photos

27 **Returning PPOW, Travis Air Force Base, Fairfield, CA**
Sal Veder
1973, © Sal Veder/Associated Press

28 **Daughters of Charity, St. Louis, Missouri**
Bert Glinn
1964, © Burt Glinn/Magnum Photos

29 **Untitled**
Harvey Stein
1978, © Harvey Stein

30 **Boys Will Be Boys**
Lisa Tichané
2015, © Lisa Tichané

31 **England, Dulwich Park**
Chris Steele-Perkins
2005, © Chris Steele-Perkins/Magnum Photos

32 **Provincetown, MA**
Constantine Manos
2015, © Constantine Manos/Magnum Photos

33 **Yugoslavia, Serbia**
Nikos Economopoulos
1995, © Nikos Economopoulos/Magnum Photos

34 **France, Maternité de Sèvres**
Valérie Winckler
1983, © Valérie Winckler

35 **Harlem 110th Street, Festival for the Police**
Raymond Depardon
1981, © Raymond Depardon/Magnum Photos

36 **Turkey, Izmir**
Josef Koudelka
1985, © Josef Koudelka /Magnum Photos

37 **Maasai on the Bike, Kenya**
Chris Minihane
2008, © Chris Minihane

38 **Boy and Dog Playing on a New Zealand Beach**
1966, © Bettman/Getty Images

39 **Untitled**
Dennis Stock
1971, © Dennis Stock /Magnum Photos

40 **Cuba**
Rene Burri
1993, © Rene Burri/Magnum Photos

41 **NYU Graduation, New York**
Richard Kalvar
1978, © Richard Kalvar/Magnum Photos

42 **Munich**
HG
2003, © HG/Magnum Photos

43 **Max and Felix**
Peter Marlow
2005, © Peter Marlow/Magnum Photos

44 **Switzerland, Lausanne. Han Suyin, Chinese-Born Writer**
Bruno Barbey
1995, © Bruno Barbey/Magnum Photos

45 **Italy, Milan**
Ferdinando Scianna
1997, © Ferdinando Scianna/Magnum Photos

46 **Smiling Monk, India**
Linda Conner
1985, © Linda Conner

47 **Beatlemania, Toronto, Canada**
Fox Photos
1964, © Fox Photos/Getty Images

48 **France**
Harry Gruyaert
1987, © Harry Gruyaert/Magnum Photos

49 **Office Party**
Leonard Freed
1966, © Leonard Freed/Magnum Photos

50 **England, Brighton Pier Horror House**
Chris Steele-Perkins
2005, © Chris Steele-Perkins/Magnum Photos

51 **Mother's Pub Outing, England**
Grace Robertson
1956, © Grace Robertson

52 **Constance, Back from the Beach**
Valérie Winckler
1989, © Valérie Winckler

53 **Constance, On Her Way to Corsica**
Valérie Winckler
1988, © Valérie Winckler

54 **Portrait of Léontine**
Jean Gaumy
1984, © Jean Gaumy/Magnum Photos

ACKNOWLEDGMENTS

Thanks to the following for their support, thoughts, and insights:

Bridget Watson Payne
Candace Fuhrman
Denise Filchner
Michael Shulman

QUOTATION CREDITS

Dickens, Charles. **The Life and Adventures of Nicholas Nickleby**. 1838–1839.

Dickinson, Emily, in a letter by Thomas Higginson to his wife recounting his visit with Emily Dickinson. c. 1870. Dickinson Electronic Archives, www.emilydickinson.org.

Begin, Menachem. Nobel Lecture, December 10, 1978. The Nobel Foundation.

Cartier-Bresson, Henri. Fondation Henri Cartier-Bresson.

Twain, Mark. **Following the Equator**. 1897.

Mother Teresa. **Catholic Online**, www.catholiconline.org.

Thich Nhat Hanh, Thich Nhat Hanh Foundation.